Tears Water
the *Seeds* of *Hope*

~ A True Story ~

Kim Tews

A Journey Across Three Continents ~
From the American Dream to Fulfillment and Joy

A special thanks to editors Jack Ferreri and Christa Ottinger Palmer
and cover artist Alfredo Rodriguez

Our gratitude also goes to internet publicist Lori Caswell.
Blog link: www.escapewithdollycas.com

CrossHouse Publishing
2844 S. FM 549
Suite A
Rockwall, TX 75032
www.crosshousebooks.com

Unless otherwise indicated, all Scripture taken from the Holy Bible, New International Version, copyright 1973, 1978, 1984 by International Bible Society. Used by permission by Zondervan Publishing House.

All stories and events described herein are true, however some names are changed to protect the privacy of the characters.

ISBN: 978-1-61315-027-6
Library of Congress: 2012944292

Dedication

To Randy—You are my hero. Thank you for making all my dreams come true! I love you.

To Mom and Dad—Your support and love have given me the courage to believe that with God's help, anything is possible. What a joy it has been to serve hand in hand with you!

Lloyd and Cleo Tindall—You have been a source of strength and wisdom that has guided and encouraged us through every step of this journey. We couldn't have done it without you.

Lauri Miro—My dear sister in faith, your love and prayers have been a lifeline. Thanks for believing that we could make a difference and for joining the charge at home and in Guatemala.

Table of Contents

Chapter One

Wrecked for Life

The setting sun painted a backdrop of cotton candy pink clouds over the roadside bar and grill where we would soon hear our favorite acoustic guitar duo sing Jimmy Buffet songs. It was an idyllic Wisconsin summer night late in June of 2005. Under normal circumstances, I would have enjoyed the warm breeze and the glow of the festive colored tiki lights on the outdoor deck with the sense of carefree recreation that midwestern families enjoy when school is out and the days are longer. Randy shook his head, smiling as our two daughters took turns throwing harmless jabs at one another, each laughing hysterically at her own jokes. I felt as if I were watching the scene from a distance, fighting back tears as my mind returned to the children I had seen two days earlier in a squalid hospital in drought and famine-stricken eastern Guatemala—a scene that would change me forever and wreck me once and for all for the relentless pursuit of the American Dream. I was haunted by the forlorn faces of two children whose hopeless situation had laid the framework for the rest of my life.

Elias, the severely starved two-year-old boy, was scarcely more than skin and bones. Hair was a luxury his body could not afford, as the nutrients available to him were barely enough to keep his vital organs functioning. His face was sunken and pale, the outline of his ribs and spine clearly visible through his thin layer of skin. He had been carried by his barefooted ten-year-old sister from El Volcancito, their remote mountain village several miles away, into the small town of Jocotan, in hopes that his life could be saved. The mother of the children was bedridden with a debilitating illness for which she could not afford treatment. My heart broke as much for the boy, barely hanging on and suffering miserably, as for the young girl, exhausted and saddled with the crushing responsibility of keeping her baby brother alive.

A frail little girl sat weeping on a tattered bench at the entrance to the facility, her body emaciated and her abdomen severely bloated, revealing the presence of parasites within her weak, trembling frame. She had been brought to the hospital for nutritional rehabilitation, and because she was four years old, and her mother had two smaller children to care for at home, she had been left alone. Lidia could not have understood why she had been left behind by her family in this unfamiliar place. She had been sitting on the bench since early morning waiting for them to return. In her hand she clutched what was probably her only toy, a comfort and reminder of home. The lump in my throat returned each time I recalled opening her tiny hand to find that she held a black plastic vulture.

Randy and I were married in May of 1993. During our early years together, we were blessed with two beautiful daughters and were pursuing careers in real estate, climbing the ranks among our colleagues in terms of sales volume. We purchased an enormous house on four acres, and although it was only four years old, we completely remodeled it to suit our tastes. With luxury vehicles and an ever-increasing income, we were living the American Dream. There was much to be thankful for, but something was missing.

Randy and I had both grown up near Madison, Wisconsin, in middle class families, Randy's Methodist and mine Catholic. We had attended Sunday services and believed in an all-powerful God, but faith and religion were not playing a major role in our adult lives. Having agreed as newlyweds to raise our family in faith, we dutifully attended services at a congregation near our home for seven years. But we eventually felt that we needed a change and in spring of 2000, we set out in search of a new church home. With no predetermined denomination in mind, we experienced a variety of church cultures, some too formal, some too weird, others seemingly insincere. We eventually stumbled across an Evangelical Free church on the west side of Madison, near our home in the suburb of Verona. I was surprised to find that instead of an organ and a choir, this church had a band that played upbeat contemporary Christian music on keyboards, guitars, and drums. The young pastor spoke with passion, bringing the Bible to life by applying scripture to issues faced by the generations of the twenty-first century. It was at this church that our faith came alive.

Our new understanding of the gift of salvation through Jesus Christ and the resulting sense of love and gratitude we felt toward God, inevitably began to pose problems for us. We were embarrassed to invite our new Christian friends to our supersized home, and conflicts began to surface in our hearts about how our time and money were being spent. One of the many bedrooms in our home had been turned into my personal closet and was loaded with clothing and shoes, most of which I did not need. I had become so busy in my career as a Realtor® that I began to feel like a gerbil on a wheel. My twelve-hour workdays did not leave room for the peace and joy I had heard should come with our newly authenticated Christian faith. One frantically busy day I decided to return phone calls while waiting in line for lunch at the McDonald's drive through. When a voice came over the speaker saying, "Can I help you?"

I was so preoccupied that I mistook it for a phone call and said, "Hello, this is Kim Tews with the Tews Team Realtors."

During the awkward silence that followed the kid must have been thinking, *"Yeah, who cares? What do you want for lunch?"*

That night I arrived home from work late in the evening to find our three-year-old daughter asleep on the couch clinging to a shirt I had worn the day before. When I asked Randy about the shirt he explained, "She said it smells like you, and she misses you."

It was time for a change.

Chapter Two

The Price of a Child's Eyesight

Recognizing our need for a vacation, we booked four tickets, packed our bags, and headed to Mexico with Randy's parents for what we thought would be a relaxing and inconsequential break from our hectic lives. The trip was a typical vacation filled with sun, fun, and sand castles, except for one thing. One day we took a van ride with several other tourists to an attraction several miles from our hotel. The light-hearted conversation between the passengers eventually arrived at the question, "What would you do if you won the lottery?" The answers ranged from sailing around the world in yachts to telling bad bosses where to go. I thought we had left our conflicted hearts at home to enjoy this break from reality, but when it was my turn to answer I heard myself saying, "I would like to make a difference for the poor people of the world."

The other passengers looked intrigued as Mike Milbach, a friend of Randy's parents, spoke up saying, "You don't have to win the lottery to do that."

The remark would have sounded condescending had he not continued in a kind tone with an invitation. "I am a member of the board of directors of a Seattle-based organization called Public Health International (PHI), and we are working in Ecuador to place drinking water systems in villages plagued by waterborne disease." He further explained that he wanted to put us in contact with a friend who would be traveling to Ecuador to visit villages that were being considered for the installation of water systems. We exchanged email addresses, and the wheels in my mind began spinning. Did he mean that he wanted us to actually go to Ecuador? That was in South America, right?

Within days of returning home I received an email from Mike's friend, Frank, a civil engineer who indeed formally invited us to join him on a trip to visit some of the poorest villages of the Santa Elena peninsula in western Ecuador.

Randy's immediate reaction was, "No way! This is dangerous territory. There are civil wars, guerillas, banditos . . ." He mentioned various other scary things that I now refer to as "monsters under the bed." But we knew that the resources God had given us were intended to be used for His purposes and, eager to put our faith into action, we offered to sponsor a water system. It was November of 2001, and we were on a plane bound for Ecuador, only a few months after the van ride in Mexico that had become the first of many stepping stones toward God's ultimate plan for our lives. We fell in love with the Latin American culture. The simplicity of the lifestyle and the kind, gentle nature of the people were inspiring, as was the gratitude they felt for the little they had. We wondered how so many in our country could have so much and be so miserable, while the people of this country could be so poor, yet so content. We had not seen the suffering of Guatemala, so with

our limited perspective, the poverty of Ecuador seemed
extreme. The idea of living without indoor plumbing alone
seemed like hell on earth to us.

On our first day on the Santa Elena Peninsula, we settled
into Manglaralto, a small oceanfront fishing town where we
would be based as we spent the next few days visiting villages
being considered for water systems. Frank took us to a local
hospital to illustrate the contrast between the health care in
rural Ecuador and that of urban America. We were appalled.
The floors of the few small dingy rooms were caked with dried
blood, and the striking lack of medical equipment and supplies
called into question what, if any, medical care could be
provided in the facility. A lone nurse passed from patient to
patient, but there were no doctors present. We happened upon
a nine-year-old boy whose eye socket was swollen to the size of
a tennis ball with infection. His mother sat helplessly by his
side in a state of despair, having been told that her son needed
an antibiotic costing nearly a month's worth of her husband's
wages, which she did not have. Without the medication, the
infection would most likely spread to the other eye, and the
boy could be left without sight in either eye. To make matters
worse, the boy's mother was living with the remorse of having
tried various home remedies that had worsened the condition.

The situation was translated to English for us since we then
spoke very little Spanish. Tears welled in my eyes as my
thoughts turned to our own daughters and how easily we
would have been able to solve this problem for them. I thought
of the life-threatening illnesses common in this country and
how often parents must watch their children suffer and die for
lack of resources to purchase medications that would have
saved their lives. They loved their children as much as I loved
mine, and it occurred to me that I had done nothing to earn

my lot in life. My life of privilege was a result of the geographic location of my birth and the opportunities that my country had afforded me. I had always been aware that thousands of children around the world died each day due to unsafe drinking water, starvation, and preventable disease. But now the problem was becoming real and personal to me in ways I could no longer ignore. Apathy, preoccupation with "the good life," and the responsibilities of home would never again be sufficient as an excuse to live as if the suffering in the world was not my problem.

The medication the boy needed was available in a neighboring town, and we asked the nurse to determine the cost and send word to us at Manglaralto's small rundown ocean front hotel where we would be waiting at a table outside. The sun was setting over the sea as a few tattered fishing boats returned to shore, their captains unloading meager rewards for a long day's work. The sound of rhythmic waves lapped upon the shore while wild dogs searched the beach for food. They, like the fisherman, survived from day to day on the outcome of their quest for sustenance.

Eventually we noticed the boy's mother slowly approaching us, her downcast eyes expressing no hope or expectation of the miracle she needed. In her hand she held a scrap of paper on which was written the cost of the medication needed to save her son's eyesight. She handed it to me without making eye contact. Twenty-five dollars was the insurmountable sum of money that would save her son from a lifetime of blindness. I stood up, reached into my waist pack, pulled out $25, and handed it to her unceremoniously. She burst into tears. Randy was next, followed by the members of the hotel staff that had been standing on the front steps of the hotel observing. As all within earshot watched in tears, the boy's mother gushed expressions of appreciation in Spanish, most of which we could not understand. Her repeated phrase, "Que Dios les recompense," were the only words I could decipher, which meant "May God repay you." After several minutes exuding heartfelt expressions of gratitude, she hurried off to purchase the medication. We were amazed to find ourselves overcome with emotion over such a miniscule contribution given at so little sacrifice. The $25 would have been spent without hesitation on a few scones and lattes back home, but here it meant the difference between vision and blindness for a child.

Evening fell, and Frank led us to the humble household of a family that had invited us to dinner, having heard we had come to help their villages. This was a large family that would have been considered wealthy in this culture, but as we entered the small dimly-lit cinder block home, we were confused to find that we were being seated at a table set for three. A mangy rat the size of a small raccoon scurried around the perimeter of the room, as Frank explained that they wished to honor us, but could not afford to feed their family the meal they were about to serve us. The fare was familiar: a small slice of beef, a mound of white rice, and refried black beans. Apparently, it was considered a privilege for this family to have us in their home, and as hard as it was to bring ourselves to eat a meal that would have been such a special treat for them, we had no choice but to enjoy their generous gift and express our gratitude for their hospitality. In reality, it was we who were honored to have been treated so kindly.

Leaving our gracious hosts we shuffled back toward the hotel, exhausted while at the same time wired from the emotional impact of the day. The next day would be action-packed, and we needed rest, but knew we could not possibly sleep. Frank bid us goodnight and disappeared to his room, so

Randy and I walked the dusty streets alone, reflecting on the day. We enjoyed the ocean air blended with the aroma of burning wood wafting from the kitchens of the humble homes that lined the streets. The world seemed to move in slow motion, and I relished the sense of peace and calm. At home I would have been dealing with the tyranny of email, paying bills, doing mounds of laundry or possibly collapsing to read a magazine, feeling lazy and guilty for taking a few moments to relax while my endless "to-do" list waited.

Eventually we happened upon a small dimly-lit tienda cluttered to capacity with snacks, cigarettes, and sundries. We bought a couple of beverages, and as we sat on the cement steps to unwind, three generations of the family that owned the shop emerged from the living quarters behind to greet us and welcome us to their town. The little Spanish I had learned thus far was nearly useless, but the five years of French I had taken in high school and college was helpful in communicating general concepts, since many verbs and adjectives are similar between French and Spanish. Randy, armed with his endearing sense of humor and a few vague memories of high school Spanish, led the conversation with a comedy of charades. The language barrier was extreme but the mutual sentiments were clear—we were happy to be there, and they were happy to have us. We had brought simple gifts: candles, nuts, candy, and Bibles which we pulled from our back packs and offered as a sign of our gratitude for their warm welcome. We laughed until we cried like life-long friends, amazed at the bond that could so quickly be formed among strangers from distant lands speaking different languages. We were having "fun" in the deepest sense we had experienced in quite some time, and, although we did not yet realize it, the wheels of change were turning within us.

Weariness finally caught up with us, and it was time to return to our tiny hotel room, joyfully exhausted, to collapse and try to sleep. As we approached the dwelling, however, we realized that our rest would be postponed a bit longer. The dark silhouette of a thin man on a bike in front of the hotel caught us by surprise. When we were within earshot, softly spoken words of gratitude poured forth from the visitor, at which point the communication barrier became a serious problem. I vowed that my top priority upon returning home would be to become fluent in Spanish. The man was the father of the boy who had received the benefits of our paltry $25 donation. He had ridden his bike into town from his mountain village eight miles away, after ten hours of work, to personally thank us for our generosity. His family had been praying for a miracle for his son, and he considered us to be the answer to their many prayers. Tears streamed from his eyes as we again heard the phrase, "Que Dios les recompensa." I wished I had been able to communicate to the man that God had paid us in advance. He had blessed our lives immensely, and we were there to express our gratitude to Him and to be a sign of His love for this family.

Chapter Three

Limited Resources and Heart-Breaking Choices

The following day was a blur of non-stop activity as we toured villages that had received water systems and wells from Public Health International. The leaders of the recipient villages proudly pumped clean water from shiny new spigots, happy to demonstrate that they were maintaining the equipment and overjoyed to have been given this life-saving gift. As we drove from village to village, we were impressed by the difference the organization was making in the health of the villagers and also taken aback by the humble nature of the small one-room straw huts that were the typical home of a family of five or six. Many traveled by horse or donkey, offering friendly waves as our truck passed. We were struck by the beauty of the landscape and the peaceful lifestyle, as babies swayed in hammocks, and children's laughter could be heard often as even the youngest ran freely throughout the communities. Men whittled tagua nuts into figurines, and women wove mats out of dried palms, both of which would be sold for income. We enjoyed every moment of our long tour during which we did not stop for meals. By the time we reached our hotel that night we were starved but still exhausted from the adrenaline-fueled sleep deprivation of the night before. We crashed without even bothering with snacks.

With the morning sun rose the aroma of a hearty breakfast prepared for us by the hotel staff. The owner of the hotel was a doctor who worked full-time in Quito, the capital city, but was on hand visiting. He offered the breakfast as an expression of his gratitude for our patronage and our concern for his people. After eating our fill we set out to visit four villages being considered as possible recipients of the water system that would be funded by the donation we had promised. We met with families, elders, and community leaders, all of whom welcomed us and pleaded for a water system for their village. Each community we toured had prepared a lunch in our honor, and in every case it was a meal that came at great sacrifice and would not have been eaten by the villagers on a typical day. Frank made the remark (in English, so as not to be understood) that when the Public Health International people visit villages, the chickens run and hide. By late afternoon, we had been served our fifth meal, each consisting of chicken and rice. Although we had no interest in more food after the third meal, it would have been a terrible dishonor to our hosts not to have eaten the meals they had prepared with such generosity. The chicken was generally served in bone-in sections that had been butchered by machete and included all possible body parts, each valuable to the villagers. On one occasion I found an eyeball staring up at me from my rice and decided that it would be less polite to eat the eyeball and then eject everything else I had eaten that day, than it would be to bury the eyeball in the rice and hope it went unnoticed.

We again arrived at our hotel exhausted, emotionally drained and facing the task of deciding which of the villages we had visited would receive our water system. It was heart-breaking. We truly believed that all human beings deserved clean, safe drinking water. The distance between the home sites in two of the villages made the installation of water systems cost prohibitive in terms of reaching the greatest number of people with the resources available. But there were two other villages that were viable possibilities based on cost-benefit analysis and the fact that the villagers had displayed a sincere spirit of collaboration in terms of their willingness to help install and maintain the systems.

During our meeting with leaders of one village in a small open air school building, I noticed a stooped figure with an apparently heavy load in tow gradually making its way up the steep hill to where we sat. As the figure neared I determined that it was an elderly woman with a bag draped over her back. I watched her for what seemed a very long time as we discussed the logistics of installing a system in this particular village. It soon became evident that Randy and I were the destination she had in mind. Again I heard many unfamiliar words in Spanish which Frank translated.

"I am the oldest living inhabitant of this village." Her voice cracked as she paused between phrases to catch her breath. "I have walked miles for many years carrying heavy jugs of dirty water to my home . . . I have seen illness, suffering, and death, much of which was caused by our polluted water supply . . . I have prayed for clean water for our children and grandchildren and dreamed of the day you would come. Now you are here and God has answered my prayers."

And with that she dropped her load at our feet. In the bag was the most generous gift she could have offered us; a large supply of a small unfamiliar fruit that she had picked by hand from a tree near her home. It was probably one of the main food sources for her family. She had been waiting a very long time for the opportunity to present this gift to the strangers from another country that could make her dream a reality. There was no way we were rejecting this village. But another village was equally feasible and cost effective.

It was time to email an update on our travels to my parents and my sister and brother-in-law, who had been praying for us daily. My sister, Lauri, had played a key role in my spiritual journey a few months earlier by sending me a copy of a book she had been reading called *Mere Christianity* by C.S. Lewis. As we read and discussed the book, we established a bond of faith, and Lauri become a source of strength that I would come to lean on for advice, prayer, and encouragement through the years that lay ahead. My parents would become another solid foundation that would be relied on for leadership, guidance, and eventually significant financial support of our work. By the time we went to sleep that evening, my parents, Lauri, and her husband Pedro, had communicated with one another, pooled their resources, and committed to the funding of a second water system.

We thanked God for His provision and traveled back to the two chosen villages the following day to deliver the news. In both cases the villagers erupted into celebratory cheers as they hugged and danced for joy. We felt as blessed as they did as we congratulated the leaders and embraced the elders. But we knew that the two villages not chosen would have to wait for other donors while they watched their loved ones suffer, and in some cases die, of waterborne disease. The feeling of joy we felt was diminished by this dilemma, which would become a struggle for us for the rest of our lives. How does one decide to help some and not others when the lives and health of so many are at risk? The need in the world is endless. The overwhelming realization that one individual, family, ministry . . . cannot solve the world's problems is the reason that many people do not get involved in humanitarian aid activities. Perhaps it is an excuse for apathy, or perhaps it is the real belief that what one can do is only "a drop in the bucket."

It would soon become imperative that we continually remind ourselves that God does not expect any of us to heal the entire world. He knows our limitations better than we do and only lays before us those tasks which He deems us capable of carrying out. He then helps and guides us, equipping us with the courage, resources, and faith to make a difference for those within our reach.

Chapter Four

Scorpions, Snakes, and Scary Roommates

Before leaving home for Ecuador, Randy and I had decided that if we could muster the courage to rough it in South America for a week, then we should treat ourselves to a little rest and relaxation at an all-inclusive resort in Costa Rica on the way home, especially since my parents were happily watching our daughters while we were away. Shortly after our arrival at the posh resort we found ourselves asking each other, "What were we thinking?" We had gone from a joyful, fulfilling, and eye-opening experience in extreme poverty to a luxury resort. Food and drink were being consumed in excess, and no one seemed to know or care about the people nearby in desperate need even in this country, one of the richest in Central America. It was like hitting a brick wall. We were miserable.

God had turned our lives upside-down and melted our hearts so that He could shape them into something useful. We were changed. We simply could not erase the images of the grass huts, the simpler lifestyle, and the fervent efforts put forth by the villagers to fulfill the dream of having something as simple as clean drinking water. As we thought of the friendship and bond we had felt with the people of Ecuador and the sacrifice of the chicken meals they had offered us, something seemed hypocritical about basking in extreme luxury only a day after leaving them.

I never got an "A" in geography, but I somehow knew we were about an hour away from Costa Rica's border with Nicaragua, a country my mother would mention during my childhood every time I did not eat all the food on my plate. I wondered if she thought that if I ate all my peas, the starving children of this poor country would somehow benefit. But because of her remarks, I had always been curious about it. We badly wanted to abandon the resort and spend our time in a place where we could make a difference. It was as if we were addicted to the incredible joy we had experienced in Ecuador. We were high on helping and craved another "fix," but had no connections in Nicaragua. We eventually realized that trying to arrange transportation and going it alone with no reservations and little Spanish-speaking ability would not only be dangerous, but completely unproductive. We resigned ourselves to the reality of biding our time in Costa Rica.

During the few months following our return home, we shared our experiences and raised support for several more water systems in Ecuador. We mentioned our curiosity about Nicaragua to our friends at Public Health International (PHI), and, as it turned out, they had friends there: two organizations similar to PHI, El Porvenir (The Future) and Agua Para La

Vida (Water For Life)—both working to install water systems in villages plagued by waterborne disease.

We began emailing both organizations and received welcoming responses. Early in 2002 we again found ourselves on an airplane to an unfamiliar land, and again Randy mentioned concerns about civil conflicts and political uprisings. But like before, I passed them off as "monsters under the bed." We eventually established a policy by which we would read the warnings on the U.S. Embassy websites for countries we planned to visit and then basically ignore them.

Carole Harper, the director of El Porvenir, picked us up at the airport in Managua, Nicaragua. She was a retired judge who had founded the organization and traveled back and forth from her home in California to Nicaragua, hosting potential donors and visiting her water projects. Carole was a delightful woman with short grey hair, a toothy smile, and story after story to tell. She paid little attention to the road as she drove us out of the city toward the rural communities of her work sites, often interrupting her own stream of dialogue to identify various bird species that came into view as we passed. The sixty-something retiree was a wealth of information as her one-sided conversation evolved from the history of Nicaragua to current issues such as the pollution of Lake Managua, deforestation, and her adopted country's political climate.

Randy and I quickly noticed differences between Nicaragua and Ecuador. I choked back the gag reflex as we passed the half-eaten carcass of a cow on the side of the road, vultures scattering briefly as we drove by. The homes in Ecuador had been artistically fashioned out of palm leaves and raised above the ground on stilts, presumably to keep them free of unwanted house guests. Amid the poverty there had been a sense of pride and decency reflected in the home settings. This was different.

Life along this Nicaraguan road looked more like a struggle for survival. Shanties cobbled together out of scrap materials such as plastic, cardboard, and rusty corrugated tin dotted the landscape. Dirt floors, makeshift latrines, and naked children offered clues as to the poor quality of life that was the norm in this region of Nicaragua.

When we arrived at our hotel we were weary from the long trip, which had begun at 4 a.m. in Wisconsin and ended late in the evening in Camoapa, a rural town several hours east of the capital city of Nicaragua. Deciding to have a beverage with Carole and the hotel staff before attempting sleep, we collapsed in a few plastic chairs in front of the hotel. Children played late into the night among the donkeys and wild dogs that roamed the dirt road in front of us. The rumbling of a truck approaching from around the corner caused us to look up, but not in enough time to avoid being doused with a pesticide being emitted to control Malaria by reducing the mosquito population. We all jumped up, coughing, sputtering, and stumbling away from the pesticide cloud. There was nothing we could do but laugh it off. We were learning quickly that a sense of humor would become an essential asset as we continued our work in Central America.

Our hotel room confirmed that the comfort quotient of the accommodations in this region of Nicaragua would be quite a bit more challenging than the adequate, but not luxurious lodging we had experienced in Ecuador. Prior to leaving home, we had been advised to bring a mosquito net, which was our saving grace. The cement block walls of the room were covered with black grime, and cockroaches scurried busily around the floor's perimeter. Spiders, army ants, and mosquitoes would also be our roommates that night. The mattress was filthy, and the pillows reeked of mold. We prayed for peace and fortitude and a coma-like sleep with the knowledge that, although we were creeped out to the max, we were basically safe. The next morning we awoke to find a buzzing creature the size of a golf ball circling our mosquito net tent. We both lay frozen, afraid to leave the safety of the mesh barrier for fear of being stung by this potentially poisonous hovercraft. But we knew we could not cower there all day, since Carole and a much-needed breakfast were waiting. I am not permitted to disclose which of us eventually had the courage to emerge from the tent and shoo the creature out the door.

It was a day much like our days in Ecuador: visiting mountain villages, learning about the organizations we would now be supporting, and making new friends as Carole introduced us to her staff. We were growing accustomed to rugged mountain travel while standing in the back of work-brigade trucks and enjoying the open air and the natural beauty of the rural terrain. During those long rides I would often thank God for the awe-inspiring journey we were experiencing. I prayed that He would continue to lead us to His will for our lives and protect us as we became involved in situations that were increasingly challenging and dangerous.

At one point on this particular trek to a mountain village, we slowed to round a corner when a man dressed in dark clothing with a semi-automatic weapon ran up and slung himself into the back of the truck with us. Randy and I were no longer alarmed by machete-wielding farmers, but this was a bit intimidating, especially since the gun was pointing upward and swinging randomly in every direction. Our host and her driver paid no attention to our new passenger. Perhaps they recognized his dark uniform as army issue or a police uniform and thought it neighborly to give him a lift. Randy made the remark that either we were in great danger or we were quite a bit safer than we had been before. At any rate, I was happy to see him hop out of the truck and go on his way a few miles up the road.

Kelly Norfield, an earthy twenty-something Peace Corps volunteer who had come to experience Nicaragua and the work of Agua Para La Vida (APLV), was riding along with us that day. She too was looking for her niche—the piece of the great puzzle that was hers in terms of making an impact for the poor. I liked her very much and enjoyed getting to know her over the course of the day. I remember standing behind the cab of the truck with her on the way down the winding mountain road late that evening, reflecting on the day and discussing anything that came to mind. With the warm wind in our hair and the open sky above dotted with stars, we were thoroughly enjoying ourselves. I spotted the Big Dipper, the same one I see from my bedroom window at home, and suddenly the world seemed very small. The sense of peace and joy I felt assured me that I was exactly where God wanted me to be at that moment. Kelly must have felt the same way as she raised her arms in the air and proclaimed, "This is the life." I agreed. I had never felt so alive. Kelly remained connected with APLV and eventually became a member of its board of directors.

We visited Nicaragua many times over the next three years serving with El Porvenir in the Camoapa region and Agua Para La Vida in the mountains surrounding Rio Blanco. Friends and family members, inspired by photos and stories of our excursions, began joining us on short-term mission trips. In addition to installing water systems and latrines, whenever we had volunteer doctors on hand we held mobile medical clinics in villages with no access to health care. We found that we could easily save lives by treating conditions such as diarrhea and pneumonia with broad-range antibiotics and anti-parasitic medications. We could ease suffering while demonstrating that there exists a love that crosses the barriers of race, class, and country to offer hope and healing to those seemingly forgotten by their own people and government. Our teams grew and word of these mission trip opportunities spread at home. Nicaragua remained our focus as the need was great and our partner organizations were equipped to handle the growing teams of volunteers that were now joining us.

Through each of these trips we became more tolerant of the difficult conditions and arduous mountain travel, as our trucks made their way up steep slopes on narrow rocky roads dangerously bordering cliffs over river gorges, often in torrential downpours. The neediest villages were the furthest from civilization, and to reach them, our teams were often forced to unload the gear and physically push the overheated mechanical workhorses up barely navigable trails in pouring rain and knee-deep mud. The equipment and supplies would then have to be carried by hand to the nearest point at which the trucks could safely haul their cargo and passengers. We relied on our faith and prayers to keep us safe and accepted only team members that had been warned of the dangers and challenges of travel to these villages, but came willingly to serve God and their brothers and sisters in need.

Several faithful supporters traveled with us frequently: Lloyd and Cleo Tindall, a retired couple from our home church; Wanda Rodriguez, a dear friend, also from our home church; Darlene and Chuck Mistretta, my parents; Dr. Tom Pasic, an ENT surgeon; and our two daughters, Allie (10) and Leah (8). This group of "frequent flyers" was an encouragement to the many newcomers who amazed us with their fortitude and willingness to deal with the challenges of travel in rural Nicaragua. The availability of electricity at our Rio Blanco hotel was sporadic at best, especially during the rainy seasons. The water trickling from the shower heads was often brown with mud, and insects of all kinds infested the hotel rooms, as did geckos and giant wart-covered frogs. It was common to encounter scorpions and snakes on our project sites, and our teams rarely ate meals at regular times. But, like us, they adjusted to the difficulties and remained committed to serving Christ in this place.

Chapter Five

Stepping Stones

Guatemala became a new destination on our travel itinerary in April of 2002 when Lloyd and Cleo Tindall were asked to lead a mission team to the country from our home church. They invited us to join them, mainly because there were no Spanish speakers on the team, and by that time I was relatively fluent. The mission trip included a variety of activities that focused on the support of a small Christian church and school. A playground was installed, teachers were trained, and friendships were formed. The team split up and stayed in the homes of families within the church—a challenging situation for those not speaking Spanish. We were the guests of a wonderful family and thoroughly enjoyed our stay with them, except for the nightly ritual of flinging cockroaches out of our bed and crushing them with our shoes before trying to sleep, knowing that their next of kin would soon be joining us.

The trip had important consequences for Randy and me, and looking back, I realize that it was most likely not a coincidence that circumstances led to our being invited along. We split off from the team briefly to meet with the directors of an organization working in Antigua, Guatemala, called The Arms of Jesus Children's Mission (AOJ). The ministry, which had been founded by Canadian Pastor Sam Martin, focused on education for children by way of a Christian school. It also provided a monthly food supply for sponsored children, as well as two-room prefabricated houses complete with furnishings to replace the poor housing occupied by most of the students' families. The Arms of Jesus Children's Mission was accustomed to hosting teams from the United States and Canada and offered many meaningful activities for those wishing to experience mission work for the first time, while making a significant long term difference for the poor of the region.

We toured Antigua and found it to be a quaint touristy town characterized by narrow cobblestone streets, a bevy of Americanized bars and restaurants, cozy inns, and rows of one-story buildings painted in colorful pastels. Horse-drawn carriages circled the central square giving visitors the feeling of having traveled back in time. Locals in colorful traditional Guatemalan garb sold crafts and souvenirs in an open-air artisan market while children too cute to refuse suckered tourists into buying cheap imported trinkets, especially near the bars late at night when they should have been tucked into bed. Randy and I enjoyed the charm of Antigua and felt that the availability of reasonable hotel accommodations, the safety of local ground travel, and its proximity to the Guatemala City airport made this town and the AOJ ministry a wonderful host for our teams and the many first time mission travelers who had heard about our trips and wanted to serve God in a developing country. We kept in touch with the leaders of AOJ and began alternating team trips to Nicaragua with trips to Guatemala to serve in partnership with them.

The AOJ ministry served as an example of how lives can be improved one family at a time through child sponsorship. Although we did not realize it at the time, our work with the organization was providing valuable training and insight that would guide us in the future. Pastor Sam Martin would become a mentor that would counsel and encourage us, sharing wisdom and offering prayer in the years to come. Randy and I, Lauri and Pedro, and my parents sponsored several families through AOJ, and as we traveled back and forth, we formed a special bond with each of them, sharing in life's joys and sorrows and praying for one another. Our children became friends and sent gifts and letters back and forth with visiting teams. We were impacted by the similarities between our families and theirs in spite of the obvious differences in affluence. These people were real. They loved each other. They strove to provide for their children as best they could. And they struggled, like all of us, with life's daily challenges.

One day we received a call from an AOJ social worker indicating that the two-year-old brother of my parents' sponsored child had died of pneumonia. His mother, Nischa, who was eight months pregnant, was blaming herself for not seeking medical treatment soon enough. She was inconsolable. Within the same month we got word that the mother of one of our sponsored families had died giving birth to her fifth child, leaving all five children and her husband to carry on without her. The oldest daughter, Lorena, dropped out of school at age fourteen to raise her siblings. These families turned to us, not for money, but for love, encouragement, and prayer. We visited them several times over the next year, mourning with them and offering hope. They knew there was nothing we could do to reverse their devastating losses, but our love and support mattered to them. Nischa named her new son Carlos after my dad (Charles), we sent Lorena to school on weekends for training to fulfill her dream of becoming a chef, and life went on. Our relationships with these families were a mutual blessing which would be remembered at an important crossroads in the near future.

Chapter Six

Crossing the Line between Faith and Foolishness?

❧

Our time at home was spent juggling the responsibilities of making a living in real estate, raising two daughters with somewhat normal lives, planning and executing frequent team trips to Central America, and raising funds for our work. I spoke at schools, churches, and Rotary Clubs in and around our home town, and mission travelers shared stories of their trips with their friends, congregations, and pastors, which encouraged more volunteers to join teams. Throughout 2003 and 2004, the frequency of the trips increased as did the size of the teams. We were inspired and encouraged by the ease with which we could recruit people from all walks of life to spend a week partnering in our work in Nicaragua and Guatemala.

I was working at home at my computer in November of 2004 when I received a most distressing call from Nicaragua. It was Reynaldo Madrid, the director of Agua Para La Vida. He reported that the torrential rains of three consecutive tropical storms in the Matagalpa Department of Nicaragua had been pummeling the mountains surrounding Rio Blanco for several days. My Spanish had improved substantially since our first trip to Ecuador, and I was able to understand the quivering voice of our friend as he described how massive mudslides had buried entire villages earlier that day. The numbers of dead and missing were unknown. Many areas were at severe risk due to the potential of future mudslides, and families were fleeing their villages and flooding into the city of Rio Blanco by the thousands. Makeshift refugee camps were materializing in schools, churches, and abandoned buildings. The need for food and water would soon become urgent, and without proper hygiene and sanitation facilities in the overcrowded camps, the spread of disease would quickly become a dangerous threat.

Tears streamed down my face as I assured Reynaldo that we would be there as soon as possible. I tried to pray but the words, "Why, God?" were all that came to mind. I desperately wanted to get on a plane even knowing that there was little we could do. This was a people that I had come to love, and I wanted to be with them in this time of crisis. I knew that making an impact would require a large team, but our usual group was not able to leave urgently, and my parents were needed at home to watch our daughters since we did not want to bring them into so risky and unstable a situation. Randy and I made a few calls to recruit help before booking our tickets. My brother, Scott, offered to go along. He had been following news of our work, but until now had not been involved. Deanna Henson, the wife of the manager of our real estate office, volunteered, also having heard of our work and wanting to be part of it. We had met her briefly at a few company Christmas parties, and I had always been impressed by her warm, friendly, unpretentious personality, an attribute that made her a welcome addition to our brave little assembly of volunteers who would soon give new meaning to the concept of loving foolishly. Three days later, the four of us were on a plane bound for Nicaragua, bracing ourselves for the scene we would encounter and the first disaster relief mission of our work in ministry.

We knew we could not bring the many tons of aid items that would be needed, but we did have some funding to commit. In those days, the airlines allowed each passenger two seventy-pound pieces of checked luggage. So our team of four filled eight oversized camouflage army duffels with clothing and antibiotics. I asked Reynaldo to gather his staff and purchase bottled water, truckloads of food, blankets, and personal hygiene items.

As we arrived in Rio Blanco the rain continued. Many villages had been evacuated, and the Rio Blanco branch of the National Red Cross was organizing relief efforts. We joined their staff, distributing food and water to the families holed up in the stalls of an abandoned flea market that served as a refugee camp. The villagers appeared to be in shock. Many did not speak at all, while those that did told stories of having watched helplessly as loved ones were buried alive before their eyes. One man had climbed a tree and managed to drag a daughter to safety while watching his wife and two sons scream in terror as they were swallowed alive by the enormous mass of mud and rock that raced by below his perch. Grief and fear hung in the air, and the sound of mourning and sorrow surrounded us.

Had this catastrophe happened in our culture, the loss of life would have been devastating, but most of us would have retained our livelihood and the possibility of replacing our homes. The victims of this calamitous disaster had lost the paltry homes and few possessions they once called their own and now had nothing to return to. They had escaped with only the clothing on their backs. The communities, the land they had farmed, the schools in which they had taught . . . all gone.

We met a middle-aged school teacher named Carmen who apparently found it therapeutic to recount her experience in heart-breaking detail. She had been away from her village during the mudslide that buried her school, but the students had been inside with a substitute teacher. All of them had been buried alive. Carmen did not shed a tear as she described her role on the rescue committee, but the pain was visible in her voice and eyes. She had been in Rio Blanco purchasing supplies, and upon hearing of the disaster unfolding in the mountains, she returned to her village to find the men desperately digging in the rubble of the school for their children, hoping to find them alive, while the women stood by sobbing. She joined the men, pulling the limp, lifeless children out of the debris one by one. There were no survivors.

Carmen went on to tell us that the survivors of her village were trapped in a mountaintop tent camp and were desperate for food and water. The camp was described as being accessible only by horseback but not more than an hour's ride into the mountains from the point at which the road ended. We discussed the possibility of bringing food, water, and supplies to them with our friends and drivers. Jaime and Sabrina were tour guides frequently employed by El Porvenir to facilitate team travel. Roberto was a truck driver and friend of Agua Para La Vida. Edwin was a well digger and employee of Agua Para La Vida, and then there were the four of us plus Reynaldo. This was a large enough group to bring substantial physical aid as well as encouragement and hope to the traumatized survivors of this village. Our Nicaraguan friends reminded us that when villagers say a trip takes an hour, it often requires three times that length of time, possibly because they lack an accurate concept of time, or more likely, because they possess a Billy-goat like quality and maintain a constant state of physical fitness that enables them to cover mountain terrain on foot at paces incomprehensible to us. Our hosts seemed less enthused about the excursion than Randy and I and our two guests did, due to the continuing rains and the instability of the terrain. I have been blessed with a husband who shares my sense of adventure for worthy causes, and Scott and Deanna apparently trusted us to make this decision. Our local friends may have been wiser, but perhaps reluctant to squelch our enthusiasm because of our financial support of the organizations they worked for. It was decided that we would leave for the camp at daybreak.

Neither Scott nor Deanna had ever been on a mission trip before. They were, however, camping enthusiasts and not intimidated by the rugged sleeping conditions of the hotel in Rio Blanco, especially since they had been warned. What they had not anticipated, however, was the terrifying trek on which they were about to embark. At dawn the following day we made our way in pickup trucks to the grassy field along which the road ended, and horseback travel was the only option for those wishing to continue into the mountains. The men of the tent camp had travelled down to meet us with all of the village's surviving horses, which would carry not only passengers, but nearly two tons of relief aid to the camp. Some of the animals were no bigger than donkeys, and none looked particularly hearty. My brother is not a fat man, but his days as a weight-lifter were still evident in his bulky physique. He was assigned a ride that was no bigger than a carousel horse. When he mounted the animal it looked as though Shrek was riding his donkey friend. The rest of us howled with laughter as the poor little animal did all it could to rid himself of this load, including dragging Scott's leg along a barbed wire fence. We laughed until we cried, but it was the last time we would laugh that day.

When all of the horses were loaded with passengers and provisions, we began our slog to what we thought was a nearby camp. To our astonishment, the village men, whose horses we were now riding, carried the seventy-pound army duffels on their backs. The mood was light and hopeful as we ascended the steep slope feeling like Superman on his way to save the world. We had been traveling about fifty minutes when the sky began to darken and storm clouds loomed on the horizon. A flash of lightning followed by ear-shattering thunder announced the arrival of a torrential downpour. Sheets of driving rain pummeled our vulnerable group, and I felt an ice-cold river running down my back in spite of the ridiculous yellow Mickey Mouse poncho I was wearing. Within minutes we were shivering and soaked to the skin.

Until this point, Scott's jokes and typically good sense of humor had kept us in good spirits. But his mood had changed. The trail was narrowing and growing steeper, and there were points at which it bordered the edge of steep cliffs. Had one of our horses stumbled or lost its footing, its passenger would have fallen to sure death or been crushed by the horse rolling down the steep slope. Although there was no conversation between us, we all realized that we had made a terrible mistake. The men with the duffels had long since disappeared, and those of us on horseback were spaced in groups of two or three by a distance of at least a half mile by now, so a meeting was not easily arranged. I wondered if we should turn back, but according to the villagers' estimations, we should have been about ten minutes from the camp.

As we pressed on, conditions worsened. Deanna had not said a word since the first lightning bolt. The lightning and deafening thunder were now nearly constant and occurring simultaneously, demonstrating the nearness of the storm and the fact that any of us could have been struck at any moment. The horses were knee-deep in mud, and each step seemed to cause great strain for them. I wondered how long the small animals could continue without rest and water. The cliffhanger pathways were now the norm, and Scott's horse was indeed beginning to stumble. At one point his horse went to its knees and slid thirty feet downhill. Scott called out "I'm sliding, I'm sliding, I'm sliding." After which, by the grace of God, the horse stopped and stood to its feet, still on the path but dangerously close to the edge of a thousand-foot drop to the valley below. I suggested that we dismount the horses and walk as close to the mountain wall as possible to avoid a plunge to sure death.

"I'll take my chances with the horse," was Scott's short answer.

I realized that he was irate with me, and I didn't blame him. I feared I had made the worst decision since the beginning of our ministry and had placed myself, my brother, Deanna, and many others in danger because of my overzealous enthusiasm for reaching these disaster victims. As the rain continued, the threat of another mudslide in this unstable region loomed heavy on our minds. I prayed continually for God's protection.

The trek may well have been an hour's ride in good conditions, but only after three hours in the most treacherous of conditions did the camp come into view in the distance. We approached the grungy assemblage of royal blue tents, and having anxiously anticipated our arrival, the inhabitants of the camp ran out to greet us. The images of hope and gratitude in their eyes upon seeing help arrive will be with me forever. The bedraggled villagers were mud-covered, worn, and weary, still reeling from the emotional trauma of recent days and mourning the loss of loved ones. They had lived through an unimaginable nightmare, and seeing help arrive from the small town miles away must have been of great comfort to them.

After a brief greeting offering our friendship and giving God the credit for our safe arrival, we unloaded the horses and organized the supplies that Reynaldo and his staff had purchased. We were stunned to find that the eight army duffels, conspicuously clean and free of mud, had arrived and been placed in a neat row. We stared at them, dumbfounded, realizing that the thin-framed men we had seen carrying them on their backs at the start of our journey had not only beaten us by a long shot, but had navigated the precipitous trails without ever having set the heavy packs down, lest they be covered with mud. I believe I speak for at least the four Americans in admitting that we felt like a batch of lazy loafers, having arrived exhausted aboard the villagers' horses, while they schlepped our burdensome bags on foot at breakneck speeds.

We went from family to family distributing clothing, water, food, personal hygiene items, and even toys. Of those who had lost family members, some wanted to share their stories, while others were content with just a hug or handshake and a word of prayer. The sense of community was striking to us. The group resembled a large extended family, each sharing a deep concern for his or her neighbors. The children ran from tent to tent as if visiting aunts and uncles. These were good, hardworking people, and I again wondered why God had allowed this to happen to them. I would continue to struggle with this question in various situations for years to come.

We treasured our time with these gentle, loving people, but as the day wore on, images of the ride to the camp flashed back in our minds. Families were still waiting to be served, and we picked up the pace of our distribution hoping to finish and be on our way to avoid making the treacherous return trip in complete darkness. We had been soaking wet for hours, and dusk brought a chill to the air. It occurred to me that I was shivering and that hypothermia could become a concern for us on the long trip back to the road. By the time we finished with the families, it was indeed nightfall.

We left antibiotics and other medications with the camp leaders to combat disease until the evacuees could be relocated and promised to alert the Red Cross as to their needs and location. A feeling of dread came over me as I mounted my horse, knowing that this poor creature would have made the entire round trip twice that day by the time it reached home much later that evening. It had rained ceaselessly since our arrival, so the paths along the cliffs would be yet more dangerous, and the night sky lacked even the faintest glow as the moon and stars were obscured by the heavy cloud cover.

Before I reached the treacherous path winding down the mountain to the road where our trucks presumably awaited, a young man in his late twenties appeared on a horse and asked me to hand him the reins to my horse. I did. He was what some might have referred to as a "knight in shining armor." He owned one of the horses that had carried supplies up the mountain with us but was not needed to carry our small crew back to the road. Yet he had decided that he and his horse would make the trip down again with the sole purpose of guiding my horse along the dark narrow paths to the road far below as a gesture of gratitude for our willingness to help under such challenging and dangerous circumstances.

There was another such angel for Deanna. My college days had afforded me plenty of experience riding horses through which I had become proficient at navigating by the use of reins, but the blessing and reassurance of a guide who knew the trail in pitch darkness was indeed a gift from God. Scott and Randy followed closely behind us, and at one point along the way, the moon peered out from behind the thinning clouds, and stars began to appear. In time I saw the lights of the trucks in the distance, and tears of relief and gratitude began to flow down my mud-covered face. I realized that we were going to make it back to the road, our hotel, and eventually home, alive and well.

Although we each retreated to our showers and beds that evening without many words, Scott and Deanna awoke the next morning cheerful and triumphant, declaring that the journey had been a once-in-a-lifetime experience that they would repeat if given the chance. Apparently they had forgiven me for risking their lives and scaring them half to death, or at least they were pretending to forgive me. As for me, although I strongly believed that those families deserved our help, and as much as I cherished the opportunity to serve and encourage them, I also believed that we are given intelligence, wisdom, and discernment as a gift from God to enable us to make wise choices. Had one of us plummeted to an untimely death that day, our ability to serve Christ and our brothers and sisters in this world would have come to a rapid end. God can protect us, but we have a responsibility to act prudently and to carefully consider His will, especially when the lives of others are in our hands. This was one of those times when it was difficult to hear God's voice, and I had my doubts as to whether or not that excursion was part of His plan.

Upon returning home Scott made a DVD of the photos and video he had taken during the trip and set it to the song "Up Where We Belong" by Jennifer Warnes and Joe Cocker. Through the images of the DVD and the song lyrics, it became clear to me that for a day, or even a few moments, a glimmer of hope had broken the darkness for those desolate souls; encouraging them, not in the knowledge that all was well, but rather through the demonstration that they mattered and were not alone. For only God could have ordered and delivered a two-ton care package from a small town in Wisconsin to an isolated refugee camp in the mountains of Nicaragua.

Chapter Seven

Seeing is Believing

❧

It was April of 2005, and we were on what would become
our final team trip in partnership with AOJ when a
conversation ultimately led to an abrupt change in the
direction and focus of our work in Central America. It was the
last night of this particular trip, and the team members had
finished dinner and retired to their rooms while Randy and I
helped the hotel owners clean up. Lionel and Rita were in their
early forties, owned several hotels and a few clothing shops in
Antigua, and would have been considered extremely wealthy
for Guatemalans. They were relatively new Christians, on fire to
serve Christ and share their faith. The casual conversation over
dish drying focused on the work we were doing through the
AOJ ministry. The couple congratulated us on our efforts and
went on to inform us that children were dying of starvation at
rates as high as thirty-three percent a year in villages of the
southeast corner of the country near Guatemala's border with

Honduras. Our chins dropped. It must have taken several moments before either of us spoke again. We were horrified.

Eventually the questions came to us. Is anyone doing anything about it? Is the government aware of the situation? What is the cause? Have you been there? Have you seen this? Randy and I wondered how it was possible that children could be dying of starvation five hours by airplane from our own refrigerator. Why had we not heard about this before? Frankly, we didn't believe the stories. We had seen plenty of poverty, but we had never seen a starving child. Furthermore, the villages of Guatemala we had seen were far better off than those we had visited in Nicaragua. We bid our friends farewell and flew home with the team the following morning.

With a cup of hot coffee in hand, I sat down at my computer and googled Chiquimula, Guatemala. The reports of drought and famine were numerous. In fact, almost everything that I could find about this department of Guatemala told of hunger, poverty, chronic growth-stunting, and high child mortality rates.

Lionel and Rita were raised in the Chiquimula Township, which was relatively affluent. But the mountains of this department of Guatemala were extensive and speckled with poor, remote communities of Mayan descent, mostly Chorti. Deforestation caused by slash-and-burn farming methods and long-term drought in this region, called "The Dry Corridor," had caused food shortages over a period of more than ten years. The shallow soil, rocky terrain, and steep incline of the mountainous land made food production difficult. A short rainy season once each year enabled the population to grow crops, mainly corn, sorghum, and black beans, and the food was then rationed until the following rainy season. But for many, it simply ran out. The rainy seasons of some years were torrential and severe, resulting in crop damage.

So our friends had been right. Once again I felt the urgent need to get on a plane. Randy was handling more of the field aspects of our real estate transactions by now, showing homes and meeting with clients. I focused mainly on advertising and office work, promoting our business from home, while networking with our partner ministries and churches, planning and preparing teams, writing speeches, and raising funding. Having just returned from Guatemala, Randy could not leave again. He had appointments and commitments, and it was important for him to continue to earn income to pay the bills and make our mortgage payments. My time away from work was taking a toll on our productivity and income, but I wanted to see for myself what was happening in eastern Guatemala and felt that I needed a travel companion if I was going to face what I feared might be devastating. I called my mom.

My father is blessed with extraordinary intelligence and has enjoyed an extremely successful career as a professor of medical physics and radiology at the University of Wisconsin-Madison. He is the developer of numerous scientific breakthroughs that have revolutionized the field of medical imaging, and his hard work has led to financial resources that have been very generously shared and invested in the lives and activities of his children. Although his career has provided travel opportunities that have taken my parents to every corner of the globe, the travel was of a different nature than what they were now experiencing with us in Central America.

One of my favorite memories of my mother's introduction to mission work was in a remote mountain village where we were offered chicken soup that we knew was made with treacherously unsafe water. We could not turn it down because of the sacrifice that killing a chicken would have been for our hosts. The soup was served in plastic bowls with no utensils, which meant we were to drink the broth and eat the chicken off the bones using our fingers. I bit my lip to conceal the laughter that welled up inside me as my mom glanced over at me as if to say, "You're kidding, right?" I slipped her a capsule containing the broad-spectrum antibiotic we often used to combat food and waterborne illness in these situations, and it was bottoms up with the soup. I was as proud of her at that moment as she was of me the first time I jumped off the diving board into the deep end of a swimming pool.

By the time Darlene received my phone call that day during the summer of 2005, she had been on many trips and had, like us, become a broken heart for the plight of the poor. When she heard my voice on the phone she knew she was going to be on a plane soon, especially since the conversation began with "I have just learned that children are dying . . ." We bought our tickets and boarded a flight to Guatemala.

Our hosts for this trip were none other than Lionel and Rita. They were happy to leave Antigua and their lucrative shops and hotels to make the five-hour trip with us to their hometown at the foot of the mountains that housed poverty, desperation, and apparently, starvation. We had communicated with them by phone regarding our desire to help, and they were eager to put their faith into action and brainstorm with us as to how we might begin. It was late when we arrived at the airport in Guatemala City. Since Antigua is only a forty minute drive from the city absent of daytime traffic, we spent the night in one of their hotels and departed early in the morning for the five-hour road trip that would take us to Chiquimula. I had given Lionel and Rita a CD of our favorite Christian music before leaving them a few days earlier, and it was playing in their van as we headed back toward Guatemala City and eastward toward Chiquimula. From the back seat, my mom and I could hear one of our favorite old hymns playing, and bracing ourselves for what we might encounter, we joined hands and listened to the words.

Here I am Lord, Is it I Lord?
I have heard you calling in the night.
I will go Lord, if you lead me.
I will hold your people in my heart.

Lionel and Rita had arranged for us to begin our time in southeastern Guatemala distributing food in a community near the bustling township of Chiquimula. Their goal was to give us a sense of the extreme hardship the region was facing. The Tierra Blanca community, which was relatively close to the Chiquimula Township, served as a convenient opportunity to assess the nutritional status of a sample of children during our first distribution of clothing, food, and toys, which had been announced in advance to summon the families. The villagers passed politely through the stations of freebies while we carefully observed. I was not the least concerned about the health or condition of the children. Some of the adults carried cell phones, a clue that we were in the wrong place. We quickly learned that those living close to Chiquimula had access to health care and employment and were doing quite well. The *city* of Chiquimula itself is quite modern and well-off as Central American cities go, but the remote *mountain communities* of the department struggle for survival on a daily basis.

The following day we made the forty-minute trip from Chiquimula to Jocotan and Camotan, sister townships geographically connected and characterized by run-down buildings, chicken busses, and indigenous peasants traveling by horse and donkey. The trash-lined streets were speckled with filthy barefooted children narrowly dodging busses and tuk tuks as they ran unattended among vehicles manned by seemingly indifferent drivers. We passed an open-air market, gagging and covering our faces with our hands, a late and ineffective defense against the putrid stench of rotting meat and fish laid out on tables in the morning sun. It was not long before the reality of the poverty, famine, and suffering became heartbreakingly evident. We were told there was a government-sponsored facility in Jocotan called, in Spanish, the Centro de Recuperación Nutricional (CRN). It was an inpatient rehabilitation center for children considered by doctors to be in "code red," or life-threatening malnutrition.

It was here that we had encountered Elias, the severely starved and dehydrated two-year-old boy carried in from his mountain village by his ten-year-old sister who hoped that doctors could save his life by treating the diarrhea that had afflicted him for weeks. It was this place that my heart and mind could not erase that summer in the carefree atmosphere of the restaurant Randy and I and our daughters would visit near our home a few days later. Cage-like metal cribs lined the walls of the dingy two-room facility. The smell of urine and feces hung heavy in the hot humid air. Tiny emaciated bodies lay on thin filthy mattresses, as mothers hunched in plastic chairs fanned their severely starved children, swatting flies and wiping sweat from their foreheads.

The lump in my throat and tears welling in my eyes became difficult to conceal and a glance at Mom revealed that she too was struggling to maintain her composure. We recognized the urgent need to step outside and collect ourselves before our emotions created an embarrassing debacle. We were strangers in this culture who looked, sounded, and dressed oddly to the indigenous parents of these fragile patients. The mothers had been watching us with curiosity since we arrived, and had we collapsed into a puddle of distraught grief in front of them, alarm and fear would have resulted. We did not exchange many words outside the CRN, but rather embraced and resolved to get a grip on ourselves, knowing that our work with AOJ and our partners in Nicaragua would soon fade behind us in the rear view mirror of our future in southeastern Guatemala. We missed Randy as we huddled behind the building with a sense of heartbroken helplessness. But then it occurred to me that, had God not brought us to this horrible scene of human suffering, He could not have convicted us to serve Him in this place. The tears we cried would soon water the seeds of hope that would change the future for children like Elias.

We pulled ourselves together and forced ourselves to carry on. This was to be a short fact-finding trip, and there was no time for us to be consumed with sorrow and grief. We needed to put our emotions on hold and function on autopilot, maximizing the productivity of the precious little time we had to learn and observe. There was one doctor and one nurse on duty at the CRN that day, and each was welcoming and informative. Dr. Juan Gandara, the staff pediatrician, gave us a tour of the small building and told of the gross lack of equipment and supplies. Babies and toddlers dressed in rags could be seen with diarrhea running down their legs. There were few medications other than a bottle or two of fever reducer, and we were told that the government budget for this clinic was so inadequate that even food for the malnourished children was often in short supply. Most of Dr. Gandara's patients suffered serious health problems as a result of their malnutrition, and children that could not be saved did not ultimately die of starvation, but rather, of diarrhea or pneumonia as their frail bodies fell victim to infection easily.

Children were often brought to the facility for help only after it was too late because toddlers under the age of three were required to have a parent or older sibling accompany them in the nutrition center. The nutritional rehabilitation is free and the companion family member receives meals during the child's thirty to sixty-day stay but is forced to sleep on the cement floor or in a chair due to the lack of accommodations. This makes it difficult for parents to fulfill their commitment to stay the full course of treatment. The presence of infants and other siblings needing care at home prevents many families from seeking life-saving attention for those determined to be at risk. In other cases, parents are not aware that their children are in grave condition, as one of the symptoms of severe protein deficiency (kwashiorkor) is swelling in the limbs, which can be mistaken for chubbiness. To make matters worse, parents are accustomed to seeing malnourished children in their villages, so many of the warning signs that would look alarming to us—thinning hair, sunken face, discolored skin—look normal to them.

We asked questions, listened, and took in as much information as we could until we feared we were taking up too much of Dr. Gandara's time. Thanking him, we promised to keep in touch and exchanged phone numbers. Our remaining time was spent interviewing locals and researching potential partners in the region before beginning our long journey back to Guatemala City and home to Wisconsin.

Chapter Eight

New Directions and Uncharted Territory

⁀

Although Randy had not been along on that first trip to Chiquimula in 2005, he understood why I was not myself that summer night at the restaurant, as we waited for the music to begin. The girls ordered burgers and fries and eventually went off to the sand volleyball pit, while we talked about the future. Randy had only heard stories and seen photos, but he was sufficiently convinced that we needed to move quickly to get involved in eastern Guatemala. The two days that Darlene and I had spent in Jocotan talking with locals had not turned over any stones in terms of identifying organizations in the area with whom we could partner, as we had in the past. It was becoming difficult to ignore what we feared God might be calling us to do. In order to make a significant, long-term difference in the lives of the people of this region, we would need to establish our own 501(c)(3) non-profit organization and set up shop in Jocotan.

The conversations of that night and the following days were a seesaw of excitement and enthusiasm, balanced with fear, feelings of inadequacy, and very real concern about our own finances. Much of my time was already being volunteered in partnership with other organizations, and although I still worked promoting Randy's real estate career behind the scenes, business was declining because the housing market had begun its descent as the recession loomed on the horizon. The booming sales and inflated home values of the early 2000s had begun to swing in the opposite direction. We knew that our work with our partners in Nicaragua would have to come to an end. Establishing and directing an international ministry would even further reduce my ability to generate income. Randy and I discussed the possibility of moving to Guatemala, but we had concerns about the disruption of our daughters' lives and friendships and the fact that the majority of the funding for our work thus far came from our efforts in real estate sales. That well would quickly run dry if we lived outside of the United States. Furthermore, other sources of support generated by the fund-raising, grant writing, speaking engagements, and networking I was doing would need to continue if we were going to make a significant difference in Guatemala.

Another factor would soon begin to take a toll on us financially. Our daughter Allie was now finishing seventh grade, one of her most challenging years thus far in public school. Although she was a beautiful and athletic teenager, the "popular" girls at school had been making fun of her. She had played competitive basketball since third grade, was an outstanding player, and was awarded the Most Valuable Player medal the prior year by her sixth-grade coaches. She tried out for the seventh-grade program, which due to volume, consisted of an "A" team for the higher skill level girls and a "B" team for the less experienced players. She came home crying one day because she had made the "A" team but so had all the popular girls who had been tormenting her mercilessly. She would rather have played on the "B" team with her friends who were referred to as "geeks," but knew she needed to play with the more competitive group to reach her potential and prepare for high school basketball.

One day she arrived at practice in a new pair of basketball shoes that were apparently "uncool" because they didn't cost $120, as did those of her peers. One of her teammates taunted her saying, "Eewww! Those are your basketball shoes?"

Without a moment's hesitation Allie had looked her in the eye and said, "Eewww! That's your face?"

Upon arriving home that day, she told me the story. The Christian in me should have said, "Allie, that was an inappropriate response. You lowered yourself to her level."

But I could not keep a straight face, and the mom and friend in me, knowing she needed acceptance and reinforcement, threw both palms up in the air for a high five yelling, "That's my girl!!!" and we howled with laughter.

Considering the horrors we had seen in Guatemala, Allie's situation seemed trivial. But she was *our* daughter and was now entering the notoriously difficult teenage years. Our girls were already making sacrifices for the ministry, and we knew that our work in Central America, like any other occupation, could potentially interfere with our attention to the details of their lives. We vowed not to let that happen. The meanness and heckling of the girls at school were taking a toll on Allie, and she had begun to go from "Princess Pink" to choosing black t-shirts and skeleton emblems as if in self-defense to say to the other girls, "Don't mess with me." It was time to get her out of there.

Months earlier, a real estate client lost her husband in a terrible car accident. She had mentioned to me that she could not have made it through the tragedy without the love and support of the families at the Christian school her children attended. It now occurred to me that if the community at this school was as caring and loving as this woman had described, then alienating and heckling a so-called "geek" would have been out of the question. The school was forty minutes from our home but I asked Allie if she would like to visit the middle and high school campuses during the spring of her seventh grade year. She agreed. As we walked the halls with our guide, we ran into Jason and Aaron, two boys that Allie had met at a youth group conference that winter. They asked her what she was doing there, and she told them she was thinking about coming to the school the following year. They looked at her and then at each other and simply said, "SWEET!!"

It was not long before the girls basketball coach heard that a tall, talented player was considering the school. He called our home and invited us to join his family for dinner. His daughter, Brittney, and another team member were on hand, and before long they were inviting Allie to summer social events. To our great relief, our daughter was back to pink and polo shirts and had decided to transfer to the Christian school by the end of that summer. Leah, our younger daughter, was about to enter sixth grade at the school that her sister was now leaving. But before the start of the school year, she announced that she too would like to go to Allie's new school. We were relieved that Allie would have a new start and happy that Leah would also be receiving a Christian education. But the tuition and travel costs would take a toll on us financially as the girls continued there into high school.

The decisions our daughters had made that summer were not the only ones that would be pivotal in our lives. During those summer nights back in Verona, the faces of the starving children of Guatemala continued to appear in my mind and dreams, as if pleading with me to do something. I knew the real estate market would recover some day, but my own feelings of inadequacy about leading a ministry in a foreign country were very real. We had few contacts in eastern Guatemala, little knowledge of the region and cultural climate, minimal start-up funding, and an overwhelming amount of poverty, suffering, and desperation to face. And then there was the daunting legal process of establishing a limited liability situation and petitioning for non-profit status with the United States Internal Revenue Service. Until now, the funding we had been raising from outside sources was receipted through our partner organizations which already had 501(c)(3) status. We could not expect donors to support our work as an independent ministry unless we had the ability to issue tax-deductible receipts.

I was overwhelmed, but I thought about a sermon I had recently given to recruit team members for a short-term mission trip and decided I should practice what I preached. I had referred to the Old Testament passage in which God called Moses to lead his people out of Egypt. Moses made excuses, citing his slow speech and basically alerting God to his obvious error with the roughly translated response, "You've got the wrong guy." But God would not take "no" for an answer and told Moses He would send helpers. I was reminded of the faithful helpers that had been by our sides in Central America for the past five years.

Randy and I called a meeting at our home summoning my parents, Darlene and Chuck Mistretta, Lloyd and Cleo Tindall, Wanda Rodriguez, Tom Pasic, and my sister, Lauri Miro. Darlene and I recounted the details of our recent trip and shared photos of the children that had stolen our hearts. We discussed the difficult long-term issues affecting this region of Guatemala and how they might be addressed. We brainstormed, shared ideas, and prayed. As the meeting came to a close, Randy and I looked around our living room at the faces of these loyal and beloved family members and friends and said:

"We are setting up shop and starting a ministry in Guatemala. We would like you to serve as the founding members of our board of directors." Each accepted without hesitation.

We had not yet established the roles that each member of the brand new board of directors would play, but Darlene, having owned two businesses in addition to helping manage the business side of Chuck's dealings, immediately engaged in the arduous process of obtaining non-profit status with the IRS. She contacted Tom Zaner, an experienced attorney who had helped others in this regard. Based on past experience, he warned her that it was a long and arduous process. We would be required to complete a two-inch stack of forms and submit our work history and an ominous list of other documents, after which the IRS typically returned applications repeatedly, requiring yet more information and clarification. He advised Darlene that the whole process would take about a year. Our hearts sank. How many children would suffer and die while we were trapped in a sea of endless paperwork and waiting? I understood that granting a ministry the right to issue tax-deductible receipts opened the door to serious fraud, and I believed that applicants should be screened carefully, but time was not on our side in terms of the urgent needs in southeastern Guatemala. We conceded that sitting around lamenting the process was not going to save any lives either, so we forged ahead.

After considering dozens of potential names for the ministry and making sure we were not using the name of an existing ministry, we became frustrated, as most were taken, and we were running out of ideas. We wanted to use words like *hope, outreach, mission,* and *world* but every combination of them was taken except "Outreach for World Hope." I think we were just plain worn out by the time we agreed upon that name because to this day I am not sure it makes much sense. But I was more concerned about the work we would do than the name of the ministry, so we decided to use it on the IRS application. I worked on the stack of forms obsessively and hated every minute of the process, but I did nothing else during the days that I had the paper nemesis in my possession because, as far as I was concerned, I was the hold up until all had been turned in to the IRS. Tom Zaner guided us through the process, suggesting revisions to our answers to make them clearer and more informative in hopes of avoiding the usual pattern of rejection and resubmission.

When I finally finished and all board members had reviewed and signed the final mountain of paperwork, we sent it off to the IRS. We prayed that the process would move along quickly and asked for prayers from everyone we knew. Then we waited. Three weeks later, on August 5, 2005, I received a phone call from a representative of the IRS:

"Congratulations, you have been approved as a 501(c)(3) non-profit by the United States Internal Revenue Service."

I phoned our now official board members with the good news. We had passed an important milestone. But it was just the beginning. In front of us remained an unfamiliar and perilous mountain. We would set out together, arm in arm, helping each other along with the power of Christ to guide us and give us strength.

Chapter Nine

Where to Begin?

Randy, Darlene, and I were off to Guatemala once again. There was much to be done. Lionel and Rita had agreed to be the organization's coordinators in Guatemala and would be working as volunteers, traveling back and forth from Antigua to Chiquimula as they, like us, needed the income of their current endeavors. We would need to hire a social worker, rent office space, and begin to network with local government and medical personnel to determine our best course of action. Our first priority would be to save the lives of children at imminent risk. We would then eventually engage in activities that would provide hope for a different kind of future for the families of this region.

Randy and I have never been known for doing anything on a small scale. During the infancy of the ministry we began to sense that the leadership of a permanent and growing operation in Jocotan was more than Lionel and Rita had bargained for, given their responsibilities in Antigua. Their enthusiasm fizzled quickly. They politely bowed out early in the process, leaving a gaping hole in the groundwork we had laid for the ministry. We were left without leadership in Guatemala and had no prospects in terms of identifying a qualified coordinator. We appreciated all that Lionel and Rita had done thus far and completely understood their decision, given their many commitments. But this was one of those experiences that one hopes is a bad dream that will fade away with the morning light. I was at Lauri and Pedro's house in Indiana working on grant proposals when I received the news. Had it not been for my sister's moral support, encouragement, and prayers, I might have turned on my heels and run for the hills.

The search began for new leadership in Guatemala. We understood that we were looking for a needle in a haystack: a servant-hearted Christian with business savvy, a love for the poor, and the willingness to work for next to nothing. By this time we had hired a social worker named Lucinda Oloroso, whose home had become the one bedroom in a small house we rented as our office in Jocotan. Lucinda had been called a social worker by her former employer only because she had played that role with love and compassion and was effective in her job. She had never received any formal education or training in the profession, nor did she have any real qualifications for running the business side of a ministry. But she eventually became our coordinator by default. A few of our board members expressed concern about this; however, we saw Lucinda's desire to serve, her genuine love for the poor, and her eagerness to learn as valuable qualifications. We could afford the meager sum that Lucinda would accept as her starting salary and believed she could be entrusted with money, an important and rare quality in a culture with a 'survival of the fittest' mentality.

Dr. Juan Gandara, the physician in charge of the Centro de Recuperacion Nutritional (CRN), became a valuable ally. We were very new in the area, and he was a reliable source of information. He was humble and appreciative of our friendship and support and would eventually look to us for help periodically when food supplies for the children ran out. We would be serving thirty-two rural villages surrounding Jocotan and twenty-nine such villages within the mountains of Camotan. The patients at the CRN came mainly from those two municipalities, with a few coming from the neighboring townships of San Juan Ermita and Olopa. Children identified as being in "code red" status were admitted to the CRN for nutritional rehabilitation by way of a few avenues. In some cases, parents would bring children to the adjoining outpatient "Centro De Salud" (health center) for treatment of illness, and doctors there would identify them as being severely malnourished and admit them to the CRN. In other cases, parents, village leaders, or neighbors of malnourished children would refer them or bring them in, having recognized the severity of their condition. Others were sent to the center by the Chiquimula Public Hospital which, having treated them for various health conditions and injuries, recognized their need for nutritional rehabilitation. Our concern, which was shared by Dr. Gandara, was that children receiving nutritional rehabilitation would return home to the same conditions that had led to their severe malnutrition in the first place. In fact, Dr. Gandara had seen many patients admitted for nutritional rehabilitation more than once.

We thought of our special connection with the families we sponsored through The Arms of Jesus Children's Mission and decided that offering individual donors the opportunity to support specific families and follow their progress would be a two-way blessing. The child sponsorship program we would soon begin would provide a monthly food supply to the newly rehabilitated children and their families, as well as follow-up medical care after returning home from the CRN. Outreach for World Hope would become a source of referrals to the CRN as staff members and visiting teams routinely visited remote mountain villages to host mobile medical clinics during which "code red" children would be identified, transported to town, and admitted to the CRN. Conversely, the CRN would refer children admitted through other sources to OWH, so that upon release, they would not be on their own to return to malnutrition.

We rapidly enrolled children into what we now refer to as the Life Boat Program through which at risk children are photographed, profiled, and provided with food supplies until they are eventually chosen by sponsors, becoming part of the Virtual Village Child Sponsorship Program. Upon beginning our work in Jocotan, we erroneously focused on a few needy villages, distributing food, vitamins, clothing, and Bibles and providing medical care to all. But we quickly came to the conclusion that there was a great disparity among the families in terms of standard of living within each village. For example, two parent families with a small plot of land were relatively self-sufficient, while single parents with several young children were clearly engaged in a daily struggle for survival. Motherless families were common due to high maternal mortality rates resulting from unattended births on the dirt floors of rustic village homes miles from help when complications arose. High teen pregnancy rates, abandoned mothers, and widows increased the prevalence of single parent families. The Virtual Village program was designed to identify the neediest of the needy in each village and reduce child mortality by accepting only "code red" children. After release from nutritional rehabilitation, these children would live in their own villages with their families, but would also be members of a "Virtual Village" through which the entire household would receive food and medical care.

Our partnership with the CRN continued, and the reciprocal referral of children grew. Forty families were enrolled into the sponsorship program during the first year. The highest incidence of starvation in children occurred during June, July, and August after the food harvest of the past September and October had run out. This became alarmingly evident during our first year at work in Jocotan. By July of 2006 the CRN was filled to capacity with children that resembled living skeletons. We were profiling them and enrolling them in the Life Boat Program faster than we could find sponsors for them. This took a financial toll on the ministry and required me to spend a great deal of time at home raising funds and seeking sponsors.

Our enthusiasm and perseverance during the long hours of work and travel were fueled by the now tangible evidence that we were making an impact as "before and after" photos of children within the Virtual Village depicted not only the difference between starvation and health, but between desperation and hope. With God's help, we seemed to be doing something right in spite of our inadequacies and inexperience. The frequent short-term mission teams became a source of financial support and child sponsorship, as well as encouragement and renewed enthusiasm for Randy and me. Volunteers came from all walks of life—some stay-at-home moms who arranged child care to travel, others using precious vacation days from their careers as doctors, nurses, construction workers, grocers, mortgage lenders—it didn't matter. All were welcome, and all had something to offer: a love that was not earned or necessitated by family ties, but that drew them into something bigger than themselves and compelled them to leave their jobs, families, and homes in search of a way to matter for those in desperate need of hope. They moved mountains with their courage, compassion, fortitude, and generosity, loving each other as they loved the grateful recipients of their many blessings.

Chapter Ten

Real Monsters under the Bed

As the ministry grew it became necessary to hire additional staff members. Randy and I traveled frequently to interview and select employees. Although we could offer only a small salary, there seemed to be no shortage of qualified servant-hearted workers interested in the jobs we offered. We had many applicants for every opening. However, the problem turned out to be keeping them. While we were at home, Lucinda was firing them one by one for their insubordination and lack of respect for her. We suspected that, although Lucinda was caring and servant-hearted, she did not have the educational background and leadership skills to manage employees and had therefore adopted a leadership style that was aimed more at maintaining control than fostering a spirit of teamwork. We prayed for her constantly in hopes that she would learn by experience. Eventually we acquired a few stable long term employees: Olivia, a high energy nurse's assistant in her forties with long jet-black hair; Erica, a petite nineteen-year-old who had earned a teaching certificate but was willing to work in ministry; and Isabel, a quiet woman in her late forties who was hired to clean the office, but eventually became involved in all aspects of the ministry's operations. The three became like sisters, supporting each other and working long hours together, often in extreme heat and difficult conditions.

Word of the ministry spread throughout the needy communities of the mountain region, and requests for help were ever-increasing, making it difficult to know when to say yes and when to say no. Our primary focus was malnutrition in children, but in spite of our clear criteria that enrollees in the Life Boat and Virtual Village programs be in "code red" status as determined by medical personnel, parents of children with other life-threatening illnesses approached us constantly. Who could blame them? If my child was dying and I could not afford the medical care needed, I, like them, would travel miles on foot carrying my sick child to town based on a rumor that a ministry from a foreign country might be the answer to my prayers. We simply could not turn away children that we knew would die without our support. By the end of the summer of 2006, there were numerous families depending on OWH for transportation back and forth to Guatemala City for specialized medical care not available in the Chiquimula region. Cases of diabetes, convulsive disorders, hydrocephalus, HIV patients requiring monthly anti-retroviral medications, a teenager with Hepatitis C, cancer patients, and villagers with other bizarre diseases too numerous to mention could not be left to die without treatment. These families, most of which were illiterate and had never traveled outside of the Chiquimula region, required escorts to navigate the many busses and the entire day's trip from their villages to Guatemala City. With one of the highest violent crime rates in Central America, the city is dangerous and intimidating. Two staff members often accompanied the families for safety in numbers.

As crisis after crisis came our way, our staff handled one situation at a time, calling me at home in the United States for guidance, encouragement, and authorization of funding for urgent causes not within our operating budget. One evening a family from our Virtual Village program knocked on Lucinda's door in the middle of the night. She opened the door to find Celia, the sponsored two-year-old girl, draped over her mother's arms, bleeding from the head. She had sustained a serious machete wound which had been inflicted by her drunken father who was attempting to strike the mother, Francina. The terrified woman had fled the village with Celia and her other young children and had made it into town but had no way of transporting the bleeding child to the Chiquimula Public Hospital, forty minutes away.

Francina was a tiny woman who made no eye contact when spoken to. She carried the weight of the world on her slender shoulders, and although she was only twenty-six years old, her tired eyes and weathered skin gave her the appearance of a woman in her forties. Her life of hardship had taken a toll on her, and we guessed this was not the first time she had fled her abusive husband. Now she stood on our doorstep in the dead of night with her severely wounded daughter, three other children, and nowhere to go. Lucinda arranged transportation and emergency treatment for Celia in the Chiquimula Public Hospital, which allowed the entire family to stay until we convinced the mother that she should not return home, but rather take refuge in an apartment that we rented and furnished for her in Jocotan. The police were notified of the incident and Francina feared her husband would find her and retaliate, a valid concern. We wondered how long Francina could bear to live in hiding, separated from her neighbors and the open-air rural setting to which she was accustomed. With no source of income and four children to provide for, she was like an animal in a trap, with no escape but a return to a home where she and her children were not safe.

Francina's situation was common in the region we served, and we realized that an enormous need existed, not only for shelter and refuge for victims of abuse, but for emotional support and rehabilitation, as well as job skills training and child care options. But all of this was beyond the scope of our ministry, and we needed to focus on malnutrition and medical care at least until we had clear leading from God that it was His will that we attempt to tackle domestic violence, displaced families, and the long road to independence for these women.

On another occasion I received a call from Lucinda while in a location of very poor cell phone reception. I couldn't hear a word she was saying. Ten minutes later I received a call from Darlene.

"Lucinda is frantically trying to reach you," she said. "It's an emergency. A four-year-old girl has died."

That was all the information she had. I don't mean to sound cold, but as I scrambled to get to a better location and call Lucinda back, I couldn't help thinking, "This is extremely sad, but if the child has died, why is this an emergency?"

When I finally connected with Lucinda I learned that the child had died at the Chiquimula Public Hospital. The staff had told the family that if they could not come up with a casket by sundown, the body would be burned with the trash that evening because they could not release it without appropriate containment. So having just lost a beloved child, the family would be deprived of the traditional nine-day mourning and burial ritual in the village with neighbors and loved ones. It was four o'clock in the afternoon, and Lucinda was calling for authorization to buy a casket.

"Yes, and please hurry!" was my answer.

After that we urged Lucinda to make these decisions, up to a certain dollar amount, without my help or authorization.

The next phone call I received from Lucinda was of a different nature. She was calling to inform me that it had become necessary for her to flee Jocotan. A nine-year-old girl had been found dead on the side of a road leading to a community we served, her internal organs having been removed from her body. An investigation was underway, and there had been no arrests, but a rumor had begun in the mountain communities to the effect that an American organization had been killing children and harvesting organs for sale within the United States. The accused organization was not ours, but we all agreed that it would be prudent to close the office to ensure the safety of Lucinda and the staff until the case could be solved. Rumors among uneducated populations are difficult to set right. A few weeks later two Guatemalan women were eventually blamed for the crime, one of whom was burned vigilante style in the streets, the other placed in jail. The founder of the accused American ministry aired radio broadcasts in an attempt to educate the public as to her innocence, and chaos eventually ebbed to calm in Jocotan. Lucinda returned and took measures to further secure the office building that doubled as her home, but the reality that violence was a way of life in Guatemala resurfaced frequently.

Several months later Lucinda would again flee Jocotan in the midst of mass rioting over rumors of a local political issue that would never have affected ninety-nine percent of the perpetrators. The municipal building was burned to the ground and, with it, a beautiful library that had just been inaugurated for the villagers' use through the tireless efforts of Jana Allen, a young Peace Corps volunteer from the United States. Jana was in despair as she learned that her year-long project had been reduced to ashes over the course of an hour. She left Guatemala, and although she was a friend of OWH, several attempts to reach her with words of encouragement were unsuccessful. It was as if she had disappeared, having lost the desire to advocate for the poor of Guatemala. She had become despondent, perhaps concluding that her hard work had been in vain, and a year of her life had been wasted because of the careless destruction brought about by the very people who would have benefitted from her efforts. Poverty breeds calamity that begins with ignorance and spawns a sense of hopelessness seemingly impossible to overcome.

Shootings took place frequently in the streets of Jocotan. One night the owner of a hotel near our office was murdered for reasons that were never uncovered. I thought back to the first days of our work in Ecuador and Nicaragua and the imaginary "monsters under the bed" that we had feared. It occurred to me that here these monsters were real, and that for the families we were now serving, they took many forms— hunger, illness, violent predators, and even members of their own families.

Chapter Eleven

An Olive Branch for Oscar

❧

OWH continued to grow and expand its reach, earning the respect of locals and villagers while being drawn into increasingly bizarre and perplexing situations. During a team event in a church late one afternoon Rosa Morales, a nurse from the CRN, entered the building, out of breath and clearly upset. I was sharing a message with the congregation when she motioned me to the back of the church with urgency. I left Lucinda in my place to finish the message and rushed to see what Rosa deemed urgent enough to justify the interruption of a church service. She needed our help to save the life of a severely starved child who was not expected to survive the night. Oscar was a four-year-old boy who weighed only sixteen pounds when he was admitted to the CRN a day earlier. He had been profiled by our staff for sponsorship and placed in the Life Boat program.

Due to the gravity of his condition and the fact that he had severe pneumonia in both lungs, Dr. Gandara told his mother that he would not survive the night unless he was immediately placed in the Chiquimula Public Hospital. Instead of transferring Oscar to the hospital, the mother decided to take him home. The CRN was able to provide the name of the village where Oscar lived, but not the exact location of his home. Night was falling as Randy and I jumped into a pickup truck and left for the mountains along with Rosa and Brenda Johnson, an American volunteer who had been living with Lucinda for a month to serve with the ministry. Dusk dimmed to darkness, and heavy rain arrived just in time to muddy the road leading from the highway up the steep rocky climb to the village where Oscar's home was thought to be. The only light along the road was the occasional glow of a single light bulb precariously hanging from the hut of a family lucky enough to have rigged a makeshift flow of electricity from a nearby line. Our headlights guided us along the narrow winding road while intermittent flashes of lightning offered fleeting snapshots of the sparsely populated mountainside.

The daunting task of finding Oscar alive hung on the very unlikely possibility that we would happen upon a neighbor or acquaintance of his family as we stopped now and then and walked from hut to hut. I was hindered by the impractical dress shoes I had chosen before my plans to share a message in a church turned into a race against time on an impromptu search mission. The slippery open-toed sandals tried to ditch me as we climbed muddy hills and slid down others, often crossing barbed wire fences to get from hut to hut. Randy became frustrated and declared that I would no longer wear sandals in Guatemala because God cared more about my ability to rescue dying children than about how I looked while preaching. Surprisingly, we found ourselves laughing. We prayed constantly for guidance, and after what seemed like hours of searching we happened upon the hut of Angela, a middle-aged widow who recognized the name of the family. She pointed back to the road where we had left the truck and indicated that the home was on the other side and down a steep embankment. We rushed off, barely taking the time to thank the woman.

Soaking wet, exhausted, and shivering, we reached what we assumed was the home of Oscar.

"Buenas Noches," we called out.

"Bueno," returned the small voice of a child, maybe seven years old. There were two of them. The children, frightened by the abrupt arrival of foreigners, confirmed that this was the home of Oscar and led us to him. He had been left to die, shivering and whimpering in a pool of his own diarrhea with no adults at home. I felt my face turn a shade of crimson as rage threatened to preclude the diplomacy that would be required to navigate the proper course of action. Clearly this situation was not the fault of the two small children, and we were concerned for their health and safety as well. We asked them if there were clean dry clothes available for their brother. They produced a t-shirt and shorts, and we cleaned and changed the frail child, almost afraid to touch him as his bones and veins were clearly visible through his taut skin. Tears mixed with the rain on our faces, and I reminded myself that the anger that I felt toward the mother of this child was not consistent with my Christian belief that we are to love our neighbors unconditionally.

The four members of our ragtag rescue committee scrambled to establish an appropriate course of action. Randy and I knew that as foreigners in this culture, taking a child from his home without parental consent constituted kidnapping and would have put a rapid end to our ability to help other children in the future. The mother was not nearly as poor as other families in the region and actually carried a cell phone for which Rosa had the number. She dialed and handed the phone to me. When a woman's voice came on the line, I blurted out the Spanish equivalent of, "This is Kim Tews, Director of Outreach for World Hope, requesting permission to hospitalize your child." The woman was indeed Oscar's mother and would have known of our work, since the ministry was becoming well established in the region, and Oscar had been profiled by our staff and placed in the Life Boat Program the previous day. She began making ridiculous objections, the first of which was her concern that we were kidnappers from a foreign land. The irony of that enraged us further. She had left her child to die, yet was concerned that he might be kidnapped before his imminent death.

The argument continued for what seemed like an hour as the phone was passed from me to Rosa and back again, each of us emphasizing the severity of Oscar's condition and the imminence of his death if not hospitalized immediately. I used every argument I could think of which included pointing out the trauma that would be endured by the young siblings if their brother died in front of them. Oscar's big brown eyes followed the cell phone as if he understood his situation and was hopeful that we would win this battle. It broke my heart to think that he was listening as complete strangers fought for his life against his coldly indifferent mother who was supposed to love him.

As the battle continued we became aware of a figure approaching. Before long we could make out the blue dress that we recognized as belonging to Angela. She knew of Oscar's condition and had decided to join the argument against her neighbor in favor of hospitalization. More time went by, and I began to worry that one or the other of the cell phones engaged in the ongoing battle would die. It was then that we noticed another person approaching. It was Sonia, Oscar's mother, still talking with me on her phone. She looked to be in her early twenties and was healthy and well fed. Upon reaching us she went on with her ridiculous arguments, and I finally lost my patience.

"I am not leaving here without this child. You will have a highly unpleasant house guest until you agree to allow us to hospitalize him." She made no response so I continued with what I later came to feel was out of line, but time was running out for Oscar, and I was desperate ". . . and furthermore," I warned, "children are a gift, and this child has been placed in your care by none other than God Almighty. If your carelessness results in his death, you will be punished."

It was then that she decided to reconsider her options. It turned out that the whole issue hinged on the fact that she was unwilling to travel to the city of Chiquimula and accompany her child in the hospital. We were to transport our team of twenty on the five-hour drive back to Guatemala City for a flight home the next morning, but we discussed the possibility of sending them on without us. Angela was still on hand, and suddenly I had an idea. We would pay her to be Oscar's guardian in the hospital. It did not take much to secure the services of this conveniently available and also loving and caring neighbor. Outnumbered and probably intimidated by the threats I had made, Sonia reluctantly gave her consent after which we scooped up the child and hastily exited before she could change her mind. She made no offer to send anything with him, nor did she make any attempt to show affection for Oscar, despite knowing that her son was being carried off by strangers to a town forty minutes away, not knowing if or when she would see him again.

The steep hike back up the embankment to the parked truck was muddy and unpredictable. There was a trail but we were definitely not on it. Randy, who was in the lead and carrying Oscar, could not see the ground below him. He stumbled several times, running into a barbed wire fence having not seen it in advance. I was still in the ridiculous sandals and was up and down like a yo-yo. Upon reaching the truck, Randy placed the shivering child on my lap on the passenger side. We wrapped him in a dry yellow towel we found on the floor and were suddenly surprised by a faint sound coming from our tiny passenger. Oscar was chuckling! Was he happy about being wrapped in the cozy towel? Had he heard and understood the battle that had taken place in his home and felt grateful that the outcome went in his favor? We will never know. We were relieved by this show of good spirits, but he was by no means out of the woods.

There was no way of turning the truck around on this narrow muddy road that bordered the mountain wall on one side and a steep embankment on the other. Randy was forced to back the truck along the road with only the dim glow of the tail lights to guide him. I prayed that a vehicle would not approach from the other direction forcing us to proceed back up the mountain. The ride to the hospital seemed eternal. I wrapped my arms around Oscar to keep him warm; grateful for each shallow raspy breath he inhaled. His tiny hands grasped my fingers with a strength that surprised me, and I kissed his head a thousand times wishing I could instantly make up for everything he had been through. When we finally arrived at the hospital nurses moved quickly to admit Oscar and place an IV in his hand for rehydration and the delivery of antibiotics. The child whimpered in protest as they poked him many times, unable to find an adequate vein due to his severe dehydration.

When they finally succeeded and Oscar seemed to be resting comfortably, we left Angela by his side with money for several days' salary and meals and returned to our hotel to reunite with the team and ask for prayers.

Chapter Twelve

A Well Worn Path in the Sky

The next morning we flew home with the team as planned, haunted by the unsettling knowledge that we had left Oscar in a precarious situation. Work was piling up at home, so we took a few days to tend to what business we could. We enlisted the help of Darlene with our two daughters, who had been with us on the trip but needed to get back to school. We then boarded a plane and returned to Guatemala and the Chiquimula Public Hospital.

Horror would best describe our reaction upon seeing Oscar. It was the Sunday of a holiday weekend in Guatemala, and there were no doctors and only one nurse on staff in the pediatrics ward. The lone nurse had run out of antibiotics, and the only person with the key to the hospital's pharmacy was on holiday. Oscar was lying in a crib, limp and lifeless with his eyes rolling back in his head. He was unconscious. It was hard to determine whether Angela or the helpless nurse was more distraught. Two children had died the day we arrived, and one had died the previous day. The nurse pleaded for our help in securing antibiotics and fever reducers from outside sources to prevent the deaths of yet more children.

Another severely starved two-year-old boy named Nelson had been profiled and placed in our Life Boat Program a few days earlier and was now lying in a crib near Oscar, having also been transferred here by Dr. Gandara due to pneumonia. His father sat slumped in a chair beside him. The nurse suggested that the boys be transferred to a private hospital offering better care and nearly adjoining the Chiquimula Public Hospital. How we wished we had known about it sooner. We gathered up Oscar and Angela and quickly convinced Nelson's father to collect his son and join us as we literally ran to the adjoining hospital, having no idea what it would cost the ministry, but not stopping to think about it. The difference between the two hospitals was night and day, as if we had arrived on a different planet. Upon seeing the children doctors and nurses came running. They immediately concentrated their efforts on Oscar. Within minutes he was rigged with another IV and an oxygen mask, and both children received nebulizer treatments. While blood was drawn for lab tests, Randy and I stood in a corner and prayed, as usual, with tears streaming down our faces.

When the children were settled in and their care was under way, a young pediatrician approached us. He looked grim and was obviously very worried about Oscar.

"Nelson will make it," he began. "His malnutrition is severe but was short term, and he will recover. But Oscar's prognosis is not good. There is only a ten percent chance that this child will live through the night."

This seemed like déjà vu to us. Our hearts sunk as he continued, "Even if he does make it through the night, his state of malnutrition is severe and prolonged. He has permanent irreversible growth stunting and will undoubtedly have learning delays and neurological problems due to the long-term damage to his central nervous system. Whether he makes it or not, you will be required to pay for our services. Are you sure you wish to go forward with this?"

It was as if he were asking us if we thought this child's life was worth saving. We were appalled. This was not a crossroads for us. There were no decisions to be made.

"Just save his life," Randy muttered.

Our thoughts returned to the lone nurse at the public hospital and her plea for help for the other children. We rushed back to the public hospital with a scrap of paper and a pen and asked the nurse to write down the names of the medications she would need until the hospital was fully operational the following Monday. We rushed from pharmacy to pharmacy that afternoon in Chiquimula finding only a few open and buying whatever they had on hand. When we had delivered the medicines to the nurse and verified that there were no other children that might have died that night without private care, we returned to our hotel and collapsed. Our hearts were broken, not just for the dying children of this weekend, but for southeastern Guatemala and the fact that one's life was only worth what one's family could afford to pay for a hospital with any sort of effective medical care. We prayed for Nelson and Oscar and braced ourselves for the bad news we might receive in the morning.

At dawn we rushed to the hospital to find Oscar alert and sitting up drinking juice. He had made it through the night, which meant his prognosis for the next few days was one hundred percent better. We were overjoyed but he was very weak. It was not until several days later that we began to see his darling spunky little personality start to emerge. He was a survivor, and we loved his courage and will to live. He was affectionate, curious, and playful and smiled constantly as if unaware of his predicament and just glad to be alive. We wanted to take him home and give him the loving family he deserved, but he was not an orphan and we saw before us the ministry's first battle for the custody of a neglected child. The medical personnel did not regularly report abuse and neglect cases, possibly because the cases were too numerous, or perhaps because these situations can become dangerous to them as parents resort to violence upon being accused of neglect.

Fortunately, Guatemala has a branch of government responsible for the protection of the rights of children. We knew that we could not return Oscar to his mother following hospitalization. The plan for the moment was that Oscar would be kept at the private hospital until he was stable and his pneumonia and diarrhea had resolved. He would then complete at least sixty days of nutritional rehabilitation at the CRN. The problem was that his mother had already removed him from that facility once and left him to die. As it now stood, she had the right to do that again if she chose. It would be necessary to report the case to the authorities and enlist their help in protecting Oscar from a return to the hellish situation in which we had found him a few nights earlier. This battle would be long and drawn out, and it was time for us to return to our responsibilities at home. We boarded a plane and again traveled the path in the sky between Guatemala City and our home in the midwestern United States.

Our staff members were to be the warriors that would continue the battle for the life of this child. We had written a careful account of the details of the case and taken many photos of Oscar the night of the rescue, which they placed in a portfolio and took to a judge. There were several court hearings during which Sonia, now irate with us, insisted that she loved the child and wanted him at home. By the grace of God, the judge ruled in our favor and ordered that following nutritional rehabilitation, Oscar would be placed at a loving home for abandoned and neglected children in a nearby township called Zacapa, about an hour's drive from our office. This would be a new and happy chapter in Oscar's life, after he finished his time at the CRN and arrived at his new home.

During his sixty-day rehabilitation, I received a frantic call from Erica. Oscar's mother Sonia, now clearly pregnant, had appeared at the CRN and was again attempting to remove Oscar from the facility and take him home. She was engaged in an argument with the CRN staff while Erica had stepped outside to phone me for advice.

"Call the police," was my very short response. I rapidly hung up so she could do so quickly. Meanwhile I called our office and had Olivia rush the court documents to the CRN so that the police would be aware that the mother had lost parental rights. This battle again ended in Oscar's favor as Sonia was forced by police to leave him in the CRN to continue his nutritional rehabilitation. He was later moved to the "orphanage" in Zacapa where he thrived.

With each future visit we were happy to see that Oscar was growing and gaining weight. He ran to us with open arms each time he saw us, which made us feel loved and appreciated, although in reality it was probably only because we always brought him toys. It didn't matter. We had not fought for his life to win his esteem and love, but because he was a precious child that deserved the chance to live out God's plan for his future. Each time he ran into our arms reeking of pancake syrup, ever chubbier as time went on, we were recommitted to the value of every life we encountered and strengthened in our resolve to battle it out for each one, no matter how fragile. After a few months Oscar was barely recognizable as the boy that appeared in the photos from the night of his rescue in the mountains.

Social workers assigned by the court visited Oscar's family from time to time out of concern for his siblings. Sonia gave birth to another boy, and by the time he was a toddler, he had been placed in the orphanage with Oscar because he was found with severe burns covering one third of his body. Sonia said he had fallen into the fire while she was cooking, but the social workers and judge had doubts about her story. Our hearts were broken, not only for the children of this family, but also for their mother. What hellish childhood must she have had that could have led to this kind of parenting? What, if any, example of love had she had in her life, and what kind of abuse had she endured that made it so difficult for her to love and care for her own children? In spite of our continuous battles with her, our responsibility as Christians was to forgive her and pray for her.

Chapter Thirteen

Seeds of Hope

By the beginning of 2007 the Virtual Village program had expanded from forty families to one hundred and twenty families, and other programs were underway in collaboration with local government to provide sustainable pathways out of poverty that would lead to independence and self-sufficiency. We had established relationships with the mayors of the communities of Jocotan and Camotan, and we began to partner with them by funding projects that would lead to improved educational opportunities for children and adults. Our visiting teams participated in school building expansions and clinic renovations and provided hundreds of desks to replace rickety tables made of sticks, bricks, and planks. Donated computers equipped three computer labs that would teach children skills that would lead to employment.

The OWH leadership was giving much thought to the need for sustainable food sources for the individual families of the region. Through the Life Boat and Virtual Village Programs we had established a means by which at risk children could be given a life-line, but we believed in the old adage: "Give a man a fish, and he eats for a day. Teach a man to fish, and he eats for a lifetime." One day while leaving the CRN, the mayor of Jocotan asked us to go for a ride with him. We climbed into his truck and headed out of town and into the mountains. Before long we arrived at a plot of land, several acres wide, that was owned by his family. It was unimpressive in terms of its agricultural potential given the steep rocky pitch, but to our surprise it boasted abundant fruit trees that were bursting with mangos, limes, and oranges. He had taken us to the orchard in order to demonstrate that several fruit tree varieties grew in the region with a high degree of drought tolerance, requiring very little maintenance. We were astonished as we learned that the tree saplings could be purchased for only two dollars each and could potentially become a significant source of nutrients and calories for our sponsored families.

Within the same general time span, Pastor Sam Martin, founder of The Arms of Jesus for Children's Mission, emailed a link to a ministry that was making it possible for families in Africa with very little land to grow vegetable gardens year-round by way of simple drip irrigation systems called "Bucket Kits." The equipment consisted of a five-gallon bucket, four hoses (each twenty-five feet in length), and a few pieces of connective hardware. The premise was that the family could build a tripod or platform out of sticks, metal, or other materials in order to suspend the bucket a few feet off the ground. They would then fill the bucket once a day with any water they could find, no matter how clean. The water would slowly pass into the attached four hoses and leak from slits spaced at specific intervals, thereby watering the seeds that had been planted along the hoses. It was working in Africa, and we were eager to try it in Guatemala. I ordered twenty bucket kits from Chapin Living Waters, and we began installing them. They were highly successful. We were amazed to find that we could plant seeds in dry barren ground and return a few weeks later to find lush food-producing gardens.

There was yet another idea that I wished to try with our sponsored families. During our mountain travels I had noticed that some of the more self-sufficient families had small hen houses and egg-laying hens. I had our staff look into the cost of chicks at twelve weeks of age, which turned out to be minimal. A small batch of these chicks, which would eventually become egg-laying hens, could be provided to our families with little cost to the ministry given that the families were willing to fashion a hen house out of whatever materials they could find on their own. The hens would need immunizations and preventative antibiotics, but the expense would be well worth the investment to give the children a much needed source of calcium and protein.

We felt confident that each of the three agriculture projects—bucket kits, fruit trees, and hens—were feasible at the family level. And each had self-sustaining capability if provided in sufficient quantity so as to produce enough food for the family and a small surplus, which could be sold to purchase additional seeds, fertilizer, and hen feed. We further concluded that if the three agriculture components were offered together, they could provide the families with a well-balanced diet, a sense of self-esteem, and a fighting chance at independence. So the Nutritional Enhancement Triad (NET) Program was born. We began its implementation immediately, placing the elements with ten families and then gradually expanding. The total cost of providing the NET program for a family was $120, making it a tangible and rewarding way that supporters could make an impact without ever leaving the comfort of their homes.

One of the first families to receive the NET Program was headed by a bright young man named Pablo. His youngest daughter had at one time been found in code red malnutrition and was therefore sponsored and in the Virtual Village program. Pablo built a hen house that was as impressive as his own neatly constructed hut, and he cared meticulously for his hens, fruit trees, and bucket kit garden. He then volunteered his help and guidance to neighboring program recipients. We were so impressed with his success and dedication that we hired him as our first agricultural support specialist, and he began traveling from village to village to expand the program and provide field support to new families receiving the hens, trees, and gardens. Another such man named Angel, who caught our attention for the same reasons, was also hired. These two men continue to help their neighbors and surrounding communities as our dedicated employees today.

In order to handle the ministry's growing administrative responsibilities in the United States, several board members were playing key roles as volunteers, doing jobs that would have cost the ministry thousands of dollars in salaries. Darlene Mistretta, our treasurer, kept track of every receipt and expenditure, categorizing the data for annual reports and tax forms which are carefully scrutinized by donors, granting foundations, and independent third-party auditors. Cleo Tindall became our Sponsorship Director and worked nearly full-time receiving all donations and sponsorship payments, issuing receipts and thank you letters, and depositing the funds in our bank account. I focused on grant writing, speaking engagements, networking with partner ministries and churches, recruiting teams, planning mission trip activities, answering endless emails, and traveling back and forth to Guatemala. The ministry was my passion. Energy fueled by the success stories of our sponsored families often kept me working late at night and into the early morning hours. My role was exciting and rewarding as I lived out the daily details of rescues and victories, but I feared that the others would soon become weary and burned out by the mundane administrative roles they filled. God chooses His most selfless and faithful servants for roles that lack the limelight and excitement of tangible daily victories, but are equally necessary and integral to every success. The reward of the invisible volunteer is the knowledge that he or she has mattered by playing a crucial role seldom noticed by others, but dear to the heart of God.

Chapter Fourteen

From Those to Whom Much Has Been Given, Much Will be Expected

Luke 12:48

On the home front our daughters were thriving at the Christian school, but the tuition and travel costs from our home in Verona to the east side of Madison, as gas prices rose to nearly four dollars per gallon, were further straining our already challenged financial situation. The drive was thirty to forty minutes each way depending on weather and traffic, and we made the trip at least twice daily, and often three times to accommodate basketball games, practices, and social events with friends, most of which lived near the school.

We had grown to love our home, not necessarily for its size and ability to warehouse the massive amounts of donated items that were now arriving daily, but because it was where our children had grown up. We had established close friendships with neighbors and had many happy memories of precious family time and special occasions celebrated with loved ones within those walls. But we knew I would likely never return to full-time work in real estate, and it appeared to be God's will that we let go of the house we called home to downsize and move closer to the school. We believe that all things ultimately belong to God and that all we have is simply on loan to us for a while. As blessed as we had been to live in our home, it was time to give it back. We listed our home for sale in July of 2007.

The school was everything we had hoped it would be and more. The families were welcoming and wonderful, and the students were polite, well-rounded Christians, not perfect of course, but miles above intentionally hurting the feelings of another human being. Since becoming a sincere Christian, I had noticed that I cried often and easily, mostly tears of joy. Seeing student assemblies at my daughters' school begin with prayer and Christian music opened the flood gates for me, and I knew once again that we were right where God wanted us to be.

Leah played varsity basketball as a freshman, so for two years, we enjoyed watching our daughters play on the same team. One night during an uncharacteristically aggressive and highly competitive play-off game, the star player of the opposing team was injured and fell to the gym floor, not moving. During the dreadful and seemingly eternal moments that followed, a silence fell over the gym as every parent imagined the unthinkable. A doctor made his way out of the audience and across the gym floor to where the young lady lay motionless, now surrounded by her parents and coaches. Our team of girls, who moments ago had been competing fiercely against this talented player, walked over to where she lay, joined hands in a circle, and prayed. Every eye in the bleachers watched this expression of love and concern and eventually the player began to stir. Our team could easily have won the competition in the absence of that athlete, but they sent the message to everyone in the gym that the well-being of another human being was more important to them than the game. They publicly displayed their faith and demonstrated that love can trump rivalry and that they knew where to turn in times of trouble. From that point on I carried Kleenex wherever I went.

Outreach for World Hope had become a labor of love not only for us, but for our family and friends. In addition to the efforts of the board members, many repeat members of our mission teams were now making significant sacrifices and investing themselves in the work of OWH in terms of their financial support and also through their time, love, encouragement, and prayers. The ministry's extended family was ever growing, and we felt humbled and honored that our mission had become a tangible avenue through which so many could experience the joy of serving God and our brothers and sisters in need. Each team was now reaching twenty-eight members, the maximum team size we had set, so as not to become unmanageable in terms of transportation and lodging. Many teams had waiting lists in case of cancellation, and members spilled forward from trip to trip.

Occasionally a team member would ask me if it would be more valuable for them to donate their travel expenses than to show up in person in Guatemala—an interesting question. I didn't know the answer so I once polled a team asking them to think of someone who had served as an encouragement and blessing in their lives. I asked them if they would have preferred the physical touch and presence of the person or the monetary value of their time and travel. In every case it was the personal touch, the love, affection, and moral support that had mattered most.

One of the greatest joys of ministry leadership for us has been the privilege of watching God work in the hearts of the mission team members, some witnessing extreme poverty for the very first time. Their experiences and reactions are life-changing as they are forced to come to terms with the fact that those of us who are blessed have the responsibility not only to care but to share with those in need. Tears are frequent and universal among the volunteers—some irrepressible in the face of the suffering they witness, others out of the love and compassion they feel while hearing stories of courage and survival in the face of overwhelming hardship. Unexpected joy mixes laughter with tears as team members work side by side with villagers to make a positive impact in the name of Jesus with the knowledge that they will return home changed, as these families live on in their hearts. Although the responsibilities of team recruiting, training, preparation, and travel are time-consuming, sharing the opportunity to serve and opening new eyes to the needs of the poor are paramount to our mission. It is out of broken hearts and tears that emerges the compelling desire to make a difference, for some through a lifetime of mission work; for others, one kind deed at a time.

I remember the overwhelming joy I felt during a mission team trip in the summer of 2008, standing in the back of the last of five work brigade trucks loaded with our staff and OWH volunteer team members, as we ascended into the mountains to work on our projects for the day. Each truck was a rainbow of brightly colored t-shirts that bore our logo. My eyes swept from dear friends to family members—and even aunts, uncles, and cousins from Chicago who had heard of our work and joined in. My sister, Lauri Miro, her family, and a contingent of their friends from Indiana had also traveled together to serve that week. I appreciated the love and compassion that each team member had for the poor and the faith and confidence they had placed in us by joining the team. The words my father had spoken to me as a child resurfaced in my mind. "If you want to be truly happy, forget yourself and live to serve God and others." I believe he was right.

The team's focus for that day was the installation of the NET program for Marta, a young widow and the single mother of five children. In addition to the agriculture projects, a second room was to be built onto her crowded hut. We conversed with Marta, as we often did while spending the better part of a day with a family, and learned that her husband and nephew had been brutally murdered in her hut in front of her and the children, during a seemingly random massacre in the village late one evening. She had grabbed her baby and toddler and fled into the night with her three older children running barefoot alongside her. They had made it to safety, but her children were in shock over the incident and suffered nightmares and other symptoms of post-traumatic stress disorder.

We asked Marta to show us the current food supply in her home, and she pointed to a dirty plastic bowl in a corner, half full of corn. It was all she had with which to feed her family of six that day. A team member immediately committed to the $29 per month for the sponsorship of this family, and the rest of us rummaged our backpacks for snacks, producing an assortment of granola bars, trail mix, candy bars, and fruit cups. The impressive supply of food that had instantly materialized was placed in a basket for the family's use when needed, which turned out to be immediately. The children tore through the unexpected bounty on the spot, devouring every morsel and licking the wrappers. We planted Marta's garden in silence, setting the five-gallon bucket high above the ground and watching the water flow through the tubes and out into the ground. This brave young woman, left to carry on with the responsibility of raising five young children alone, could have watered the garden with the tears she had cried.

Upon returning to Jocotan that evening, a few team members asked to see the CRN where many of their sponsored children had received nutritional rehabilitation. We stopped in to find the facility loaded with severely starved children, as was the norm during the summer months. One of the children, Martilena, was of particular concern to us because she was only six-months old, and the person fulfilling the CRN's caretaker requirement was a mentally impaired teenaged girl. The child was in severely poor condition, and we wondered who was in charge of her care at home. As we suspected, it was indeed the impaired teen, not capable of taking care of herself, much less a six-month-old infant. The child's father was a seventy-five-year-old alcoholic. As the story went, the child's mother had died during childbirth and the mentally challenged teenager was the child's sister. This situation mimicked Oscar's case in that we knew that if the child was ever returned home, she would not live. We spoke with Dr. Menendez, the physician one authority level above Dr. Gandara, and implored him to contact the children's rights department and have the child placed in a safe environment. He agreed.

A week after retuning home with the team, I called our staff to have them check the status of Martilena. They visited the CRN and learned that she had been taken home and CRN staff had done nothing because her machete-wielding father had threatened to kill anyone who tried to separate him from his daughter. Locating Martilena became an urgent priority. Erica

and Olivia, probably terrified, made the trip to the mountain
village in hopes of finding Martilena alive. Upon arriving they
found her abandoned on the dirt floor of her hut, near death
and barely breathing. The photos I received turned my
stomach. The baby was naked, severely starved and dehydrated,
her tiny emaciated body covered with open sores. Although she
was too weak to cry, her facial expressions revealed excruciating
pain. To say that I was furious beyond words would have been
an understatement. I was disgusted, not with the helpless
teenager who was mistakenly expected by logical, reasoning
adults to take care of the child after she had already
demonstrated that she could not. No, I was disgusted by the
apathy of those who knew Martilena's story and had decided
that it was not their problem. Perhaps this child's right to live
was easily enough put aside in the face of the threats of a
drunken seventy-five-year-old man.

Once in our possession, the child was rushed to the private
hospital. There was no one to argue with this time, as the father
was absent from the home for weeks at a time, and we had
fewer concerns about being accused of kidnapping, having now
established ourselves in the region as a ministry advocating for
children. Again the question, "Why God?" entered my mind. It
was a question that was resurfacing in my thoughts frequently.
Why would God have created a child only to watch her suffer
and die? Had this little one passed underneath His radar? That
theory went against my belief in an omnipotent and omniscient
God. But the suffering she had endured could understandably
challenge even the staunchest Christian's belief in a good and
loving God. I thought of the massacre Marta and her children
had witnessed and survived. I thought of the starvation and
illness I had been confronting on a daily basis for years. I
thought of the tsunamis and earthquakes that were taking place

in other parts of the world. And I thought of the conversations I'd had over the years with my beloved brother, Scott, who could not come to faith because of the suffering in the world.

Chapter Fifteen

Are You There God?

Scott and I were kindred spirits during our childhood and teen years. As children we would go to a hilly, wooded nature area called Lucy Park and ride our bikes down the steepest cliffs we could find to see who could stay upright the longest. We would come home caked in mud with holes in our jeans and scrapes on our knees. As teenagers we gave our parents the ride of their lives. We seemed to be in trouble often, although we always knew we were forgiven and loved unconditionally by our parents and each other. I have always been able to share my thoughts with Scott, and whether we agreed or not, we always respected each other's opinions.

One thing that is common among new Christians is the desire to share with others what they have found in Christ. To me, understanding and accepting Christianity was like finally stumbling upon the pot of gold at the end of the rainbow, the fountain of youth, or the winning lottery ticket. I felt compelled to share the good news with everyone I knew. Scott was always willing to give me the time of day and even engage in conversations regarding his doubts. He once responded to my claim that God was in control by saying that if God was the CEO of a major corporation, His performance evaluation would lead to His immediate dismissal, as His establishment (the world) was in a state of complete disarray. There were wars, natural disasters, famines, and epidemics that threatened to wipe out continents, not to mention extreme poverty, violence, divorce, and on and on. I had to admit, he had a point.

I have heard it said that life on this earth is but a blip on the screen of eternity and that God uses our challenges in this life to build character in us. Having faced many challenges in my life, I know that each has shaped the person that I am today. I also believe that we would be like spoiled children, had we never been forced to grow in maturity and character by enduring and overcoming hardship. I understand that God is more interested in shaping us into the likeness of His Son and preparing us for eternity than providing for our comfort and ease in this life. But Martilena seemed to have been born only to suffer and die, without ever having had the chance to grow in faith or maturity. And there were thousands more like her dying every day. This was creating a serious conflict within me that I could not ignore. I believed in the truth and validity of the Bible, but one passage was becoming a formidable stumbling block for me:

> [25] *"Therefore I tell you, do not worry about your life, what you will eat or drink; or about your body, what you will wear. Is not life more important than food, and the body more important than clothes?* [26] *Look at the birds of the air; they do not sow or reap or store away in barns, and yet your heavenly Father feeds them. Are you not much more valuable than they?* [27]

Who of you by worrying can add a single hour to his life? [28] *"And why do you worry about clothes? See how the lillies of the field grow. They do not labor or spin.* [29] *Yet I tell you that not even Solomon in all his splendor was dressed like one of these.* [30] *If that is how God clothes the grass of the field, which is here today and tomorrow is thrown into the fire, will he not much more clothe you, O you of little faith?* [31] *So do not worry, saying, 'What shall we eat?' or 'What shall we drink?' or 'What shall we wear?'* [32] *For the pagans run after all these things, and your heavenly Father knows that you need them.* [33] *But seek first his kingdom and his righteousness, and all these things will be given to you as well."*

Matthew 6:25-33

Could we tell the people of Guatemala not to worry about what they would eat? Could we tell the people of Nicaragua and Ecuador not to worry about what they would drink? Many of those we had served in Ecuador, Nicaragua, and Guatemala had been seeking His Kingdom and His righteousness. Many were sincere Christ followers, yet it was clear that "all of these things" were not being given to them. It was becoming increasingly difficult to reconcile a loving God with the suffering I was encountering. I remembered the joyful, faith-filled months following our experience at the new church years earlier and wondered if we had made a mistake. If God was good and loving while at the same time ever present and all powerful, why had He not answered the prayers of these faithful hard-working people?

I also remembered our successful years prior to really *knowing* Christ and recalled the feeling that we were somehow missing the boat. Children were dying then, just as they were now, while we obliviously increased our wealth. It occurred to me that perhaps the starvation in the world was not God's fault. He had created a world in which there was enough food to go around more than once. But it was not evenly distributed. God gave us free will, and as a result, we live in a broken world where there is greed, corruption in government, overconsumption by those living well, and apathy toward the plight of the poor. Perhaps it is not God who is responsible for the hunger in the world.

I wanted so badly to explain away my doubts but what about the mudslides of Nicaragua? Many had died instantly. Surely God was not attempting to build character in those that were lost in the massive rivers of mud and rock that had buried their villages. Throughout the history of mankind there have been tsunamis, earthquakes, and tragedies of every kind which have raised the same questions. Why God? Certainly human greed and apathy could not be blamed for the suffering caused by these events. I continued my search for answers, realizing that I was not willing to give up the faith that had been the source of so much joy.

I heard on the news one morning, when our country was deep in mourning and sorrow after the events of September 11, 2001, that church attendance was soaring and Bible sales were increasing at astonishing rates. The tragedy had reminded our country of its need for God. America had been attacked on its own soil and was no longer an untouchable fortress immune to attack from the outside. A people, reeling in the aftershock of unthinkable tragedy, resorted to faith and prayer.

The devastation of hurricane Katrina created a mission field for thousands of people who were now taking their first mission trips and finding faith and healing in their own lives, while at the same time sharing hope with others and establishing a love for serving God and their brothers and sisters in need. A year after Katrina ravaged several cities of our Gulf Coast, it was nearly impossible to throw a rock in our home town without hitting someone who had traveled there to help its victims. Stories of new faith and the joy of serving filled communities throughout the United States.

Hundreds of people have been blessed and changed for life by the mission field they have experienced with us in Guatemala. A successful business woman joined a team because she felt a lack of meaning and fulfillment in her life. She was one of the top mortgage lenders in our community—well-known, respected, and making a huge amount of money. Yet she felt that something was missing. Her trip to Guatemala was life-changing. She never returned to her career in mortgage lending, but instead, enrolled in nursing school and went on to address the AIDS crisis in Africa. God had used the famine in Guatemala to shape her into something He could use for His glory while at the same time filling her with the fulfilling life He had planned for her.

This is not to say that there are not countless secular careers filled by hard-working people bringing glory to God through tireless dedication to their important roles. But at times God uses specific circumstances to effect change in our lives and to call us to the purpose He has planned for us. We each have different but important batons to carry as members of God's relay team. Sometimes the hardest part of joining the team is identifying which baton is ours to carry, be it in our own household, our hometown, or on the opposite side of the world. This is why God often uses heart-breaking situations to help us identify our batons.

I concluded that God can bring good out of tragedy. If we believe that He is omnipotent and is ultimately in control, then we have to believe that He allows tragedy because He thinks that the good He can bring out of it is worth the suffering that it causes. I am not callously attempting to minimize the suffering of those left in the wake of enormous catastrophes. Most of those in the midst of hardship and loss as a result of these tragic events would be appalled by the idea that God was using them to draw others to Himself and His purpose. My theory would not seem fair to them, nor does it to me. No one can claim to have all the answers. But we must come to terms with the fact that the word *faith* itself means believing in things that we have reasonable cause to accept as true, even though there is no proof. If we could knock on heaven's door and simply ask God for the answers to all of our questions and doubts, then our trust in God would not be by faith, but by knowledge. We have incomplete understanding by our nature as human. If we presume to comprehend all matters of God and eternity from our limited perspective, then we are like the ant that thinks all there is to the universe is what he can perceive.

So I chose faith. I had seen God at work in many ways. I had seen miracles and answered prayers. I had felt God's leading and presence throughout our journey, and I had seen Him call laborers to join us in His mission field. At the end of the day, I continued to believe in an omnipotent, omniscient, good and loving God.

Martilena's case went through the court system, and she was placed at the same Christian home for abandoned children that was loving and caring for Oscar. The plans God had for her life had only just begun to unfold, and we had no choice but to trust that His plans were perfect. There was much to be done, and another phrase had become words to live by for our ministry: "Onward Christian Soldiers."

Chapter Sixteen

A Rainbow for Luis

Las Minas was the mountain community that would be the focus of our visiting team's mobile medical clinic and distribution in April of 2008. We arrived to find the usual sea of brightly-colored traditional Mayan Chorti dresses partially obscured by babies slung over the shoulders of mothers who had already been waiting in line for hours by the time our trucks rumbled up to the school at 8 a.m. The team worked swiftly to unload and categorize donations in the two-room building, creating an efficient assembly line process by which volunteers would serve one family at a time as they passed through the aisle. Some would dispense medications to eliminate worms and parasites; others would outfit children with age-specific and gender-appropriate clothing and shoes. Vitamins, toys, stuffed animals, new underwear, and Bibles would also be distributed. Our youngest team members initiated ice-breaking activities with the waiting children, using bubbles, balloons, and kazoos to put the timid crowd at ease, while offering proof that Americans could be playful, warm, and even comical. The medical team created a triage area to screen for severe malnutrition and illness requiring antibiotics or specialized medical care. These were always special days of fellowship and community for the villagers as they gathered with their neighbors in hopes of receiving basic life necessities and health care, and for most children, the first real toy they would ever own.

I am often questioned about the prudence of expending valuable resources and luggage space for the provision of toys to children. In response, I tell the story of a family road trip that ended in trauma for our daughter, Leah. We packed up our hotel room, doing a final sweep in search of stray socks and toothbrushes, before locking the door for the last time and checking out. Fifty miles down the road it occurred to Leah that Beacon, her beloved teddy bear and best friend of three years, was not with us. Panic ensued. This bear had helped Leah through life's ups and downs including the typical colds and coughs, a rare skin disorder, surgery to remove a tumor from her foot, and countless other stressful events. She simply could not live without the bear and was quickly becoming hysterical. We had no choice but to take the next exit and double back to the hotel where we found Beacon tucked comfortably underneath the top layer of blankets where Leah had slept. Once reunited with her tattered furry soul mate, all was well in Leah's little world again. The bear was a source of comfort for her during life's trials and heartaches. These children deserved the same, in slightly better form than tiny plastic vultures.

I gave a brief greeting to the waiting crowd, expressing our gratitude to God for the privilege of serving our brothers and sisters in this beautiful country. Pastor Gudiel, a charismatic preacher who often tagged along on our missions to share the

Gospel, took his place on the cement wall surrounding the school and bellowed out his message while the women listened, glad for the entertainment if for no other reason. Many of them were Catholic, some Evangelical; most had at least a basic belief in some sort of God. My role at the distributions was best described as troubleshooter and translator, since most team members did not speak Spanish and struggled to understand the polite requests and expressions of gratitude of the villagers.

I was often called into the makeshift medical clinic area to make decisions about arrangements for specialized care or to profile a severely malnourished child for sponsorship. In these situations it is almost always necessary to transport the child down the mountain to the CRN or Chiquimula Public Hospital. In each case we find ourselves engaged in a dialogue in which our staff, doctors, nurses, and I patiently work to convince parents that the child is at risk and needs hospitalization. These often lengthy discussions cover the challenges of supervision for siblings at home, the need for a companion for the child during hospitalization, separation anxiety, and fear of the unknown. The indigenous families have little education, are largely illiterate, and typically do not recognize the severity of their children's conditions. The rumors of poor quality public medical care do not help our cause, nor does the fact that hospitalized patients often die, in most cases not because the hospitals fail them, but because the parents wait too long to seek help. We once took a family to court because they refused to allow us to provide surgery for a child with a large cancerous tumor growing rapidly within her cheek, lop-siding her face and making eating nearly impossible for her because of the pain.

At a distribution much like today's we had recognized the need to hospitalize a teenage girl named Anna whose face and limbs were swollen from protein deficiency (kwashiorkor). She was stunted to the size of an eight-year-old. Anna refused to come with us until Gabriela, another teenaged girl from her village, was also deemed to be in "code red" status. Gabriela fled upon learning that she needed hospitalization but returned later with a little bag on a stick, hobo style. She had changed her mind. Using the enticement of hearty meals three times a day and the fact that there was a television in the CRN, we convinced Anna to join her. That distribution ended late in the evening because we never left a village until everyone in the waiting crowd had been served. Anna sat on my lap in the back of the pickup truck winding its way down the mountain toward the distant lights of the township of Jocotan. The two brave girls were old enough to stay at the CRN alone and had therefore left their homes and families, not to return for thirty days, in the darkness of night with strangers from a foreign country.

We bumped and bounced down the rugged mountain road, the lights of the city growing nearer and brighter. Our brigade was within ten minutes of the CRN when, as if someone had flipped a switch, the entire town went dark and seemed to vanish into thin air. Blackouts were common in Jocotan and usually lasted only about an hour, but this was indeed bad timing. I noticed that my legs felt damp and quickly realized that Anna was now trembling and had wet herself. I pretended not to notice and made small talk asking Anna about her home, family, and school. She asked me why I was wearing earrings, stating matter of factly that she thought Christians were not supposed to wear jewelry. She wondered aloud why we were in villages taking children to town for hospitalization. I loved these questions because they gave me the chance to share my faith.

"We are one family with God as our Father. That makes you my sister, and I care about you. Sometimes God asks us to help take care of our siblings, just as you help take care of your little brothers."

I told her about Jesus and His love for her and before long we were at the CRN admitting Anna and Gabriela by candlelight. Anna thanked me before we left, a sign that she understood that what we had done was for her own good. The next time I saw her she was wearing earrings.

Pastor Gudiel had finished preaching and this distribution was now finally underway. I stepped outside to assess the size of the growing crowd. That way I would know exactly how much worrying to do over whether we had enough clothing, toys, and medications for everyone—something I could do nothing about other than pray for the multiplication of the fishes and the loaves. Many of the village men worked in distant townships, leaving their families for weeks at a time to earn what little they could as day laborers for the owners of larger fincas (farms) miles away. Those at our distributions never stood in line, but rather waited in the shade of nearby trees chewing grass and kibitzing. Today something caught the attention of the small group of men reclining near the school. They stood to address an approaching threat to this day of blessing for their village.

An inebriated man staggered toward the crowd, swaying back and forth as if tossed by the wind. Luis, drooling and disheveled, made his way nearer. His machete dangled loosely from his crooked belt, threatening to make him a shish kabob should he lose his balance and fall. The village men, hands on hips, formed a human barrier as they marched forward to rid the happy scene of this embarrassing menace. But they were interrupted by a crazy American woman (me) racing toward the drunkard and cutting them off before they could reach him.

"Bienvenido Hermano" ("Welcome Brother"), I blurted out, surprised by my own impetuous decision.

I placed his arm around my shoulder and steadied him as I steered him into the school building, almost overcome by the stench of his un-bathed body. The team, now aware of what was going on, cleared a space and brought a chair to where I stood balancing the pitiful soul on his rubbery legs. I often scared others, and even myself, with these abrupt knee jerk reactions, but there is seldom time to think things through in these situations. This man was probably an alcoholic because of neglect and rejection he had experienced as a child. When would it stop for him? It broke my heart to think of him trying to join the festivities taking place in his village only to be turned away, an unwanted outcast. We searched our backpacks for juice boxes and sandwiches and wiped his face with a stained and torn article of donated clothing someone had intercepted before it was inadvertently offered to a family.

Luis spent many hours in the chair that day, in the center of the action like the guest of honor, while his neighbors filed past to collect their goodies. He dozed off and on, and between snoozes ate more food in an afternoon than he typically saw in a week. The team worked tirelessly, and as afternoon faded into evening, I decided Luis was lucid enough that I could do the most important thing I would do for him. I grabbed my travel worn Spanish New Testament and read to him.

"For God so loved the world that he gave his one and only son, that whoever believes in him shall not perish but have eternal life." John 3:16

*"God shows his love for us in that while we were
still sinners, Christ died for us. Romans 5:8 (ESV)*

Luis, now sober, began to cry. I assured him of God's love
and forgiveness. I told him of the free gift of salvation and
eternal life through the acceptance of Christ's offer to take the
blame and punishment for our sins, leaving us clean and free to
start anew in friendship with God. I told Luis that he was not
alone in his condition, that we were all sinners and we all
needed God's grace and forgiveness. The team, breaking briefly
from their tasks, took to corners in groups of three or four to
pray for Luis, asking God to give him understanding and hope.

Finally, I asked Luis if he would accept a gift more valuable
than everything that had been distributed that day. I asked him
if he would place his faith in Jesus Christ. He nodded, now
sobbing. I called the team together and each member placed a
hand on Luis. As we prayed, members of the village joined us,
placing their hands on the shoulders of the team members. A
concentric circle of brightly colored OWH t-shirts and
indigenous Mayan dresses grew into a giant rainbow around
Luis, as two cultures addressed their God together on behalf of
a lost sheep, now found.

Chapter Seventeen

Searching for Rita

By the fall of 2008 the combined Virtual Village and Life Boat populations had grown to two hundred and seventy-five families. Our time at home was becoming a three-ring circus as we struggled to manage our real estate commitments, family life, our daughters' activities, and the responsibilities of the growing ministry. The massive amount of email I was receiving was sucking up my time and energy and becoming a source of dread. Sponsors, supporters, churches, mission team members, board members, partner ministries, and our staff in Guatemala were all in constant communication with me. Although I was grateful for each of them, it was overwhelming.

Then there were the emails from people who had heard of our work in Guatemala and wanted to use the ministry to accomplish their own unrelated goals, like reconnecting their Guatemalan adopted children with birthparents, providing scholarships for siblings of adopted children, and transportation of various items to Guatemala with our mission teams. I felt obligated to respond to each request with a polite "no" but resented the amount of my time this was requiring.

Another issue was mounting as an unavoidable hazard of having founded a ministry. Almost everyone we knew—from friends and family to casual acquaintances—was aware of our work, and most were contributing, at least in some small way. This was truly a blessing, but amounted to hundreds of people, all of whom had causes of their own, from cancer walks to children selling cookies. We felt obligated to reciprocate the generosity of each, worried that failing to do so would appear stingy and ungrateful. So as money flooded into the OWH account, personal income flowed out of the Tews family budget and into a myriad of causes, some worthier than others. I once gave fifty dollars to the political campaign of a child sponsor about whom I knew nothing. I later pondered the irresponsibility of that decision, considering that he might have been an advocate of animal torture or who knew what?

As the real estate market declined and a full blown recession was becoming a reality, its impact could be felt dramatically, not only by real estate agents, but also by those who were losing their jobs in all markets and fields. Many of the homes Randy was listing were in foreclosure or short sale situations, making accepted offers more time-consuming and difficult to bring to the closing table. Home values were plummeting, and sellers who bought property during the peak market, or borrowed the equity in their homes based on higher values, now owed banks more than the value of their homes. The average time on the market for homes in our area was over a year as the economy declined and buyers were almost nonexistent.

Our own home had been on the market for thirteen months with no offers. Buyers were skittish and homes with big price tags simply were not moving. Money was becoming a real issue for us, and we reduced the price of our home several times. I remember a conversation I had with a dear friend and neighbor after our home had been on the market for over a year.

"Kim," she had said, "perhaps it is not God's will that you leave your home. It has enabled you to host OWH gatherings such as fund-raisers, board meetings, mission team meetings, and reunions, and your basement is a giant warehouse for ministry donations. Perhaps God wants to continue to use *His* house in this way."

I loved both God and this friend, but I was feeling extremely frustrated at that point and felt like saying, "Well, if God wants us to keep this giant warehouse/reception hall, then He had better start blessing us with some income to pay the mortgage and taxes." We decided to take our home off the market and refinance our fifteen-year mortgage over thirty years to lower the payment, as an alternative to further reducing the price and selling it at a loss.

Our oldest daughter Allie's high school graduation was now around the corner, and she was starting to make plans for her future. Our girls had grown up, and I was feeling very sentimental about the thought of them leaving home. I loved being a parent and was not ready to become an "empty nester." I would have continued having children but was medically unable after the birth of Leah. I longed for more children and had discussed adoption with Randy in the past, but he was not interested. As the girls got older, the thought of their leaving was a source of great sadness for me. We had the ministry, which brought us joy and fulfillment, and others were telling us we had thousands of children to care for, but it wasn't the same. I had grown up in a close family, the members of which were my best friends. Our daughters, even as teenagers, were beginning to consider us their best friends. Was it wrong to want more of such a wonderful thing? The adoption discussion resurfaced periodically.

As 2008 rolled into 2009, new ideas and projects for OWH renewed our excitement and energy. I thought about the illiteracy issue in the villages we served and wondered if the women had any desire to learn to read. Erica had been trained as a teacher, but this skill was not being used through her role with the ministry. I called her and pitched the idea of a pilot reading program in Plan De La Arada and Pacren, two villages in which we had a high concentration of sponsored children. She was excited and enthusiastic about the idea, which passed through the board of directors unanimously. We set the goal of enrolling thirty women in each of the two villages. They would meet twice each week for two hours over the course of four months and would receive notebooks, pencils, and eventually reading materials. They would be required to complete homework assignments for each meeting and prepare for periodic quizzes.

Randy and I flew to Guatemala for the inauguration of the program to give the women a pep talk about the importance of literacy. We expected to address thirty women in each location, but were amazed to find nearly eighty people, including men and teenage boys, at each meeting site. We had not planned on these numbers but simply could not turn anyone away. An additional teacher was hired immediately and the program was underway with a total of one hundred and fifty enrollees.

Back at the office Randy and I sat around chatting with our staff about which two villages would be good candidates for the next round of literacy classes. We were overzealous, as usual, and fired up to eradicate illiteracy in eastern Guatemala. Our lively conversation was interrupted by a knock at the door. We opened it to find Carol Langley, a missionary friend from Colorado, with a severely deformed teenage girl named Alma, and her father, Roman. They had heard of our work and wished to speak with us. Carol lived in Jocotan part-time and taught Bible stories to young children by way of a Bible club she had started. Alma had joined her club but was often unable to attend the meetings due to back pain and almost constant headaches. The curvature in Alma's spine reduced her height by five or six inches, and her twisted torso clearly caused her physical pain and discomfort. I knew in an instant why they had come, and my heart broke as I imagined the emotional burden this young lady must be carrying as a severely deformed teenage girl.

A brief conversation revealed that Alma's severe scoliosis was threatening her life because the encroachment of her spine on her lung-space was increasing as she grew. Most cases of scoliosis are characterized by a two dimensional C or S curvature. Alma's was a three-dimensional curvature, best described as a spiral or cork screw. The family had been told that without corrective surgery, Alma would die. They had also been told that the surgery she needed was high risk and could not be performed in a developing country. This was clearly a family of scarce resources, and I imagined what it must be like for them to live with the knowledge that they would soon watch helplessly as their daughter died of pulmonary complications resulting from her deformity. Roman supported his family by diving to the bottom of a dirty river to extract sand for use by a local cement company, while his wife, Juana, made and sold tortillas to neighbors. Doctors had told Roman to do anything in his power to find a way to get Alma to the United States for surgery. They might as well have asked him to rope the moon.

Roman had been begging for help from anyone with connections in the United States but had made no progress. I dreaded giving him the same answer he had received time after time. Alma had a case of scoliosis that was likely one of the worst in history. In the modern world, surgical intervention would have prevented her deformity from developing to such an extreme degree. The cost of corrective surgery now, not to mention anesthesia, medical imaging, hospital expenses, travel, and lodging for her parents would have sent our ministry into bankruptcy. The problem was simply bigger than we were. Taking on Alma's case would have placed the health of one child above the lives of the hundreds we could have saved from starvation with the resources we would have needed to invest. Making these decisions was a reality of our work that I hated. I could not bring myself to give an outright "no" to Roman and Alma. So without making any commitments, I said I would talk to connections at home to see if there was anything we could do. As they expressed their gratitude and turned to leave I felt guilty, as if I had given them false hope just to save myself the sadness of telling them they did not stand a chance.

It had been a rewarding trip, and we had planned to leave the following day feeling triumphant and joyful. But this unexpected visit had dampened our joy, and it was not to be the only thing that would remind us that we were not in the Land of Oz that day. Shortly after Carol, Alma, and Roman departed we received a distressing call from the Chiquimula Public Hospital. An eight-year-old girl named Rita had been admitted to the Intensive Care Unit in a state of severe starvation. We were asked to profile her for sponsorship, but upon making the forty-minute trip to the hospital to photograph the child, we found that her parents had taken her home. They probably expected her to die and wanted to avoid the "body release" issue that was well-known and would deprive them of the traditional mourning process. I am afraid that this issue is responsible for many deaths, as parents refuse to take children to this hospital with the knowledge that they, or their bodies, may never make it back to the villages.

There was very little information on the location of Rita's home, and doctors indicated that she would not live for more than a day or two unless re-hospitalized. It would be another night of hiking and hut-hopping in the mountains, seeking clues that might lead us to Rita. Having little time for preparations we took to the mountains to make use of the remaining daylight in search of Rita, hiking the rocky trails until afternoon drifted into evening and darkness fell over us. I felt deflated, as if all of the joy of recent successes was draining out of me in the face of the seemingly hopeless situations of two girls whose lives hung on the outcome of our efforts. Several hours passed with no leads on the location of Rita's family, and it was pitch dark and time for Randy and me to make the five-hour trip back to Guatemala City for our flight home. We were heartsick. Our staff was to begin the search again at daybreak and was not to give up until Rita was found, but we did not have high hopes.

We arrived home as the second day of the search concluded—still no Rita. We knew that it was most likely too late but sent out prayer requests to everyone we knew. On the third day of the search our staff was given a tip from a pastor as to the location of Rita's home, and by nightfall, I received a call from an exhausted Lucinda. Rita had been found alive but her condition was grave. Our staff had convinced the family to re-hospitalize the child, but Lucinda was concerned about the ramifications for the ministry if she were to die en route to the hospital. We had no choice but to take our chances and face the consequences later. I authorized private hospital care, and Rita and her rescue crew began the trip from the mountains back into town. Rita was eight years old but could not walk. Her frail body was carried for several miles down steep mountain paths, passed back and forth between our staff and her parents as they made their way into Jocotan and on to Chiquimula. She survived the trip but her prognosis was poor. Echoing many similar phone conversations with the hospital's staff pediatrician, I heard the speech about our obligation to pay, whether she made it or not. Did he not know us by now? I wondered if he thought that one of these times I would say "Let's just let this one die."

Rita was too weak to stand even to use the restroom, so although she was old enough to be left alone, she would need a companion to stay with her. Through interviews with her family we determined that she was loved and not neglected. But there were many younger siblings needing care at home, and her mother simply could not stay with her in the hospital. A caretaker was hired to accompany Rita, and she began her recovery. Boredom became a problem even before leaving the hospital for her sixty days of rehabilitation at the CRN. Her caretaker took her for rides around the hospital in a wheel-chair, and we provided games, crayons, and coloring books to occupy her time until she was eventually mobile and strong enough to be moved to the CRN. Rita's was the longest recovery of any patient we had taken on thus far. Her family's love for her was demonstrated by their many visits to see her during her recuperation, providing evidence to us that a court custody battle was not necessary to secure a healthy future for Rita. She is now completely recovered and a sponsored member of the Virtual Village.

Chapter Eighteen

An Angel for Alma

Rita's rescue and hospitalization had restored my can-do outlook, and I remembered my promise to go to bat for Alma, as hopeless as it seemed. Leah's best friend had undergone scoliosis surgery a year earlier, and Leah and I had taken bedside shifts with her mother during her grueling recovery. I remembered the name of her surgeon, although I realized that I might as well have been the man in the moon to him. I decided I would call and ask him if he knew of any charity hospitals who took on cases involving poor children of developing countries. I had heard of Shriner's and St. Jude's Hospitals, but I knew little about them and hoped that possibly Dr. Noonan could point me in the right direction. I looked up his office number and felt completely obnoxious as I dialed it and left him a voice mail.

"I am the Director of Outreach for World Hope, working in Guatemala to . . . and I have recently been approached by a sixteen-year-old girl with a life-threatening case of scoliosis . . ."

I completed the message and hung up the phone, relieved that at least I had not dropped the ball completely. I truly cared about this girl and wanted to give her a chance, but I knew there was little hope. I needed to remind myself that this case was outside of the scope and focus of our ministry (malnutrition), and I could not expect to be able to solve the problems of every child in Guatemala. An hour later my cell phone rang displaying an unfamiliar phone number. It was Dr. Kenneth Noonan. I told him Alma's story, giving what little information I had about her health history and background. Then I paused and waited for what I thought would be his polite regrets. I was dumbfounded when the complete stranger on the other end of the line declared without hesitation "I'll do the surgery for free." He continued, "Give me four days to rally the help of the hospital and an anesthesiologist."

The rest of the conversation is a blank in my mind. Having been driving, I pulled into a parking lot and just sat there in disbelief for what must have been twenty minutes. With tears streaming down my face, I called Randy, then my mom.

Dr. Noonan called back exactly four days later having secured the volunteer services of an anesthesiologist and donation of the entire hospital stay to include two weeks in the Pediatric Intensive Care Unit and four weeks on a regular floor. Everything would be provided for Alma including the medical imaging and twenty thousand dollars worth of orthotic equipment from a company called Biomet that supplied Dr. Noonan's paying patients with the hardware needed to rebuild their spines. It seemed too good to be true, and I was almost afraid to notify Alma's family for fear that it would all come crashing down and they would be left devastated. But the pieces continued to fall into place. I contacted the Ronald McDonald House and secured lodging for Alma's parents. Next

I obtained free airline travel from American Airlines through their "Miles for Kids" program, which brings underprivileged children from around the world to the United States for medical treatment not available in their own countries.

It was time to notify Alma and her parents. Relief, excitement, hope, and tears of joy soon mixed with fear, anxiety, and apprehension as this poor humble family envisioned airplane travel to a foreign country, the language of which they did not know. The reality of the daunting high-risk surgery that Alma would face was terrifying. X-rays taken of Alma's spine in Guatemala City had already been provided to Dr. Noonan who confirmed that hers was the worst case he had ever seen. He would have to break her into pieces and put her back together again using a tool chest of plates, pins, and screws. Because of the severity of her case, it was possible that two surgeries would be required, one week apart, to complete the job. The surgeries would be extremely high-risk and the recoveries excruciating. We explained the medical risks, including paralysis and death, in detail to Alma and her family to ensure they would not make a trip to the United States only to panic and back out later. The prospect of becoming a paraplegic in a developing country with rugged terrain and humble living quarters could not be taken lightly. The family was overwhelmed, and we urged them to take some time to think and pray rather than make a hasty decision. But we all knew that Alma had no choice. To do nothing would have been a death sentence.

Carol Langley volunteered to travel to the United States with Alma, Roman, and Juana to guide them through the airports and to be their translator. She became a source of comfort and reassurance that was likely pivotal in their ability to muster the courage to commit. Soon the hopeful bunch was en route to Guatemala City to apply for passports and temporary medical visas, armed with several official letters documenting the necessity of the trip—one from Alma's Guatemalan doctor stating that the surgery could not be done in Guatemala, one from Dr. Noonan verifying that he would do the surgery for free, and one from OWH assuming responsibility for all accommodations and travel expenses not donated. They completed the required paperwork, signed with a fingerprint, as did those who could not read or write, and returned home to wait and worry. The family's two bread-winners would be out of the country for at least six weeks, leaving younger children in the care of older siblings. Although there were no "code reds" in the family, they were placed in the Life Boat Program temporarily and would receive food supplies from the ministry while Juana and Roman were away.

The surgery was scheduled for September 4th 2009. Dr. Noonan requested that the family arrive a week prior to surgery for preoperative appointments, an MRI of Alma's spine, and several lab tests. The OWH Board of Directors hosted a dinner and reception for Alma and her family, at which supporters offered a warm welcome and showered the family with gifts of clothing, pajamas, robes, slippers, and personal hygiene items for their room at the Ronald McDonald House. Time between appointments was spent touring the city of Madison which they found to be incredibly beautiful. Madison is home to the University of Wisconsin campus and boasts a beautiful downtown area built on an isthmus between two large lakes. There are endless things to see and do, especially in the still-warm and inviting climate of early autumn. The vacation-like itinerary we planned took the awestruck visitors from a tour of the capital building, to Vilas Park Zoo, to various malls and museums. Walks down the pedestrian-only restaurant-and-shop-lined State Street, followed by pontoon boat rides on Lake Mendota seemed like a trip to Disney World to the appreciative threesome given the limited range of experiences available to them near their home in Guatemala. There was little time to reflect on the gruesome weeks that lay ahead for Alma, whose attention to adjusting to a new culture provided a happy diversion. Tasks as simple as operating an elevator were completely foreign to the newcomers and required training.

One of the rental properties we owned, a two-bedroom condo ten minutes from the hospital, became Carol's home away from home. We furnished it with a bed, a couch, and a TV, and then stocked it with basic hygiene items, cleaning supplies, and easily-prepared microwavable meals. Much of Carol's time would be spent at the hospital, so this little pad would be used for little more than sleep. Carol and I picked up Alma and her parents at the Ronald McDonald House the day of the MRI and sat patiently waiting with Roman and Juana during the exam, which we were told would take about an hour. An hour and a half came and went with no news from the exam room. When the end of the second hour rolled past, we became worried about Alma's comfort, as lying for long periods of time was painful for her and made breathing difficult. At home her parents would prop her into position with pillows so she could steal a few hours of sleep at a time, relieving her from the grips of her oppressive captor, a freakishly-twisted spine.

Carol and I made small talk with Juana and Roman, who were oblivious to the fact that the exam was taking way too long. At the two-and-a half-hour mark I could stand waiting no longer and approached the receptionist. She disappeared briefly and returned with the following information:

"They have noted something unexpected and are taking care to record all of the images needed by the surgeons."

I wondered how I should translate this for Alma's parents, ultimately deciding that the only fair option was to give them complete literal translations, avoiding the temptation to sugar-coat news with overprotective optimism. Something was wrong and we needed to be in prayer.

After three hours Alma emerged exhausted and in urgent need of a restroom. The cheerful technician could make no comment on his findings, the explanation of which would be the responsibility of Dr. Noonan after careful consultation with a professional radiologist. The five of us had no choice but to shuffle off to lunch and await news. It would be the following day that we would be summoned to a meeting with Dr. Noonan and, unbeknownst to us, a neurosurgeon that had now been recruited to Alma's case. Much to the relief of Carol and me, a medical translator was also present.

"Alma has a very large oblong cyst on her spinal cord that will make surgery to correct her scoliosis prohibitively dangerous at this time." We sat frozen as Dr. Noonan continued. "The risk of paralysis should we operate in the presence of a cyst this size is statistically unacceptable." The other surgeon nodded in agreement, and Dr. Noonan finally introduced him, a hospital interpreter translating sentence by sentence.

"This is Dr. Iskandar, a pediatric neurosurgeon who has studied Alma's MRI results. There is a constriction at the base of Alma's skull that is hindering the flow of fluid between her brain and spinal cord. It is to blame for the cyst as well as the hydrocephalus that is causing Alma's frequent headaches."

Roman exhaled as if he had been holding his breath for an eternity.

Dr. Noonan continued, "My colleague is a specialist in such cases and has agreed to perform surgery at the brain stem to alleviate the constriction which may, over time, and with some luck, cause the cyst to drain so that surgery can be done to straighten the spine at a later date."

Alma, Roman, and Juana sat motionless as the translator broke the news.

"Do you have any questions?" she added. The three bewildered faces of Alma, Juana, and Roman simultaneously turned to me, their unofficial spokesperson, looking for guidance and a response. Carol shared that role but said nothing, probably stunned into silence.

"Thank you on behalf of each of us, especially Alma." I stammered, addressing Dr. Iskandar at first. This friend and colleague of Dr. Noonan had just been drawn into a heart-breaking situation involving the life and future of a destitute teenager from a foreign country and had generously offered to carry his baton, promising another major surgery free of charge. How I kept from collapsing into a puddle of tears I will never know. Although the situation was a major setback for Alma, there was hope and even a glimpse of joy in this additional display of altruistic love and generosity being poured out on behalf of the family.

The translator fluently converted English to Spanish and vice versa as we discussed the risks and recovery period associated with the Chiari Release surgery that would now be an unavoidable stepping stone to a potentially healthy future for Alma. Juana and Roman placed a disconcerting amount of value on the opinions of Carol and me, and we were both uneasy in the knowledge that they would do whatever we thought best whether we were right or wrong. But the choice was easy. We knew, as did both surgeons, that this course of action was Alma's only hope. She would be exposed to more of the typical risks associated with surgery and anesthesia and would endure yet another difficult procedure and painful recovery, but there was no other choice but to move forward with the proposed surgeries.

Dr. Taryn Bragg, another neurosurgeon and colleague of Dr. Iskandar, also agreed to participate, and both appeared in Alma's preoperative room in scrubs as nurses placed an IV in her thin arm. I had not seen Alma shed a single tear thus far, and her composure before surgery convinced me that she was as tough as they come in terms of teenage girls. Fear was an emotion she could not indulge considering the long and arduous road ahead of her. Dr. Bragg was as kind and encouraging as Dr. Noonan and Dr. Iskandar had been, and we thanked God for these three angels who would team up to offer a life-line to a most brave and deserving young lady.

Alma's first surgery was a success, and although the recovery was challenging, the family returned home triumphant, with the commitment of the hospital, the surgeons, the anesthesiologist, and OWH to see her through to the happy ending that had not been cancelled, but merely delayed. She would wait six months before another MRI would be done in hopes that the cyst had disappeared.

Chapter Nineteen

Bridging the Gap between Life and Death

Whenever the phone rang in the middle of the night I knew the call was coming from Guatemala, and I knew it was not good news. This was no exception. It was Lucinda. A woman had delivered a baby at home two days earlier and had been bleeding continuously, most likely having retained a portion of the placenta. It was not until she was near death that her husband had become concerned and decided to seek help. The lone ambulance at the Jocotan Centro De Salud was not equipped for the rugged mountain roads that led to her village and was, as usual, out of gas. Several village men had tied a blanket between two poles and were attempting to carry the woman down to the township of Jocotan on foot. En route, having realized that her death was imminent, they had called Lucinda.

Eduardo was a local man in his fifties who owned several rugged 4 x 4 pickup trucks that we often rented to transport our mission teams to project sites in villages accessible only by steep, rocky, mountain roads. I told Lucinda to awaken him and pay him to drive out and meet the rescue party and then rush the woman to the hospital. These conversations were always short. I hung up and prayed.

As I waited for news in the wee hours of that morning, I thought about the many motherless infants kept alive by infant formula provided by our Life Boat Program. I thought about the unattended home births which were the norm and the resulting maternal mortality that was devastating families. I thought about this woman's situation and other life-threatening emergencies that resulted in unnecessary deaths due to the lack of reliable ambulance service by a vehicle capable of navigating the treacherous mountain roads. It was time for a Board Meeting.

The state of the U.S. economy was taking a toll on the ministry's income in terms of support and donations, and I was about to ask the board to approve the purchase of a used 4 x 4 pickup truck for use as an ambulance, which I estimated would cost between $12,000 and $14,000. The board of directors generally shared my enthusiasm for projects that would bless hundreds of people on a shoestring, but this was an expensive proposal. I began the meeting with a suggestion that we gather and equip midwives with basic supplies such as flashlights, towels, pots for boiling water, umbrellas, scissors, plastic tarps, and suture materials. I also proposed training programs for midwives and publicity measures to encourage expectant mothers to seek prenatal care so medical staff could identify complications of pregnancy in advance of the onset of labor. We discussed the need to educate the population as to the importance of attended birth, at least by a midwife. The rescue attempt of a few nights earlier had failed, and the woman had died en route to the hospital. Her story began my pitch for the ambulance truck.

Our Board of Directors consists of wise and responsible stewards who love the ministry and the people of Guatemala. A long discussion ensued regarding the ministry's financial status, the need for a licensed driver, liability issues (not only for accidents, but for patients who would die in transit), insurance needs, and gas prices. Lucinda was in favor of the truck and pointed out that the vehicle could also be used for patient transport back and forth to Guatemala City. With a ministry vehicle, families making frequent trips to the city for specialized medical care could be combined, and the round trip could be completed in one day rather than the two days necessitated by the series of bus transfers. This would save the ministry a great deal of money in terms of lodging and meals for the traveling families.

After deliberating well into the night, the board of directors decided that the benefits of a multi-use ministry vehicle outweighed the costs and risks. Randy and I were off to Guatemala to purchase our first ministry truck and to hire a driver. Carol Langley recommended a licensed driver named Francisco who was quickly interviewed and hired. By the time we arrived in Guatemala City, he had preselected several vehicles for us to consider. Francisco and his mechanically-savvy father assisted in the selection of a tough little red Toyota pickup truck with a four-door double cab, which became the ministry's first medical transport vehicle.

The process had gone so perfectly that Randy and I had time to spare before flying home. We decided to visit Martilena at her orphanage to see how she was doing. We were amazed to find the child to be completely rehabilitated and healthy. The nourishment she had received had enabled her body to develop in the way in which God had intended. Her amber skin, now healthy, contained a plump toddler with thick, shiny curls framing angelic chubby cheeks. She was barely recognizable as the starved shell of a human infant that had been rescued by our staff.

The very being that had caused me to question my faith several months earlier now re-confirmed my belief in an intelligent creator. The complexity of the little machine on my lap with its beating heart, elaborate central nervous system, ability to see, hear, and smell, and the amazing capacity to heal itself and adhere to the blueprint built within, all pointed to something much more awe-inspiring than unguided nature. She could not have materialized by the chance union of her components any more than a toaster could assemble itself independently of a mechanically-minded craftsman, and her functioning was infinitely more impressive. She had feelings, emotions, memory, and a spirit. God reveals Himself in many ways; creation of humanity and the world around it are among the most impressive and convincing. I thanked God for her recovery and concluded that it would take the suspension of reasoning and common sense to believe in the existence of Martilena without believing in God.

We were grateful that the orphanage was taking good care of Martilena, but she deserved a family of her own. I wished we could take her home with us, but my periodic mention of adoption had been swept under the rug by Randy many times. Our daughters were in favor of a baby sibling, but Randy simply was not ready, and this was not something that could or should be forced on another person.

We had planned a two-day stop in Florida on the way home to catch our breath and delay our return to our hectic lives at home. Naples was an upscale town filled with wealthy tourists and retired Northerners who spent winters in the South. We chose it because it was a convenient drive from our Miami layover, and we had visited the area with friends in the past and had special memories and favorite haunts there. We knew we could do it on a budget. One night after eating dinner at a bargain-priced Italian restaurant, we walked down Third Avenue, a street lined with expensive restaurants and clubs for retirees. At an outdoor restaurant we watched the older crowd, dancing slowly to a Lawrence Welk style band.

"Honey, that's us after our kids leave," I joked. "Are you ready for that?" Randy rolled his eyes, and we made our way to Fifth Avenue and an Irish Bar with an upbeat live band.

"Let's do it!" he suddenly yelled over the music. I couldn't hear what he had said.

"What?" I yelled back.

"Let's do it. I'm ready. Let's adopt Martilena."

Was he serious? It was I who had been bringing up adoption for years, never really having to think through the financial implications or logistics because Randy simply wasn't on board.

"Are you serious?" I blurted out. "You can't say that unless you really mean it."

Guarding my emotions, I feared he might wake up the next morning and start back-pedaling. I could not allow myself to get excited. But he was on a roll.

"Yes. Let's do it. I'm serious. I've been thinking and praying about this, and I think we should do it."

Then he put his money where his mouth was! He texted my Mom and told her to call me right away because I had "big news." I knew he was serious at this point, and I was sobbing by the time my mom was on the phone. He meant it. We did not know whether it would be possible to adopt Martilena specifically or not. But we would be parents again to an orphan who needed a loving family. I awoke the next morning wondering if it had been a dream. I imagined all of the precious moments we would now be able to relive. There would be Santa Claus and the Easter Bunny and the wonder of watching a child experience each new chapter of life. I had never been so in love with the man who had spent the last eighteen years of his life making all my dreams come true.

Chapter Twenty

Love as a Way of Life

Upon arriving home we began to look at our financial situation and the fact that we would need to borrow money to cover the adoption fees. It was now the spring of 2010, and the economy was showing no signs of recovery. We considered the reality of another mouth to feed, diapers, and the potential of unexpected medical expenses for the child. In spite of our concerns, we had to face the fact that we were in our mid-forties and it was now or never. We simply could not wait a few years to see if the real estate market improved, as we would already be relatively old parents. We prepared a balance sheet outlining our assets and liabilities, and in spite of the several years of recession, we were managing to stay in the black. We had some equity in two rental properties which we could sell if it became necessary. The refinance had cut our mortgage payments in half, and we were willing to further cut corners to welcome a new family member into our home. Our daughters agreed and got busy planning a theme for the nursery.

We met with a social worker from Catholic Charities to begin the required "Home Study" process, which is a prerequisite for any international adoption. There were classes to take, interviews to go through, and home visits to be completed. We quickly learned that prospective adoptive parents are carefully evaluated to assess their ability to provide a safe and loving environment for adopted children. The years we had spent in ministry advocating for children were helpful in convincing a social worker and judge that we would be fit and loving parents, as did the well-rounded success of our two teenagers. The concern, possibly precipitated by adoption cases gone wrong, was that the new sibling would be rejected by our much older biological children. We were asked if there was any possibility that our teenagers would mistreat the new family member. I answered this concern with the following story:

When Allie was a junior in high school, she noticed that Mitchell, a timid blond-haired student, would eat his lunch sitting alone in a corner on the floor of the lunchroom, avoiding all contact with other students. She wondered "what his deal was" and decided to approach him one day. So she plopped herself at his side in his corner and attempted a conversation. Mitchell stared at the floor offering one-word answers to her questions in tones barely audible, making Allie feel awkward and at a loss for discussion material. The following day Allie convinced her friend David to join her on the floor with Mitchell, this time bringing their lunches, which proved to be a bit more successful, but Mitchell continued to be reclusive.

It was the day before Christmas break, and Allie had an idea. She rallied Leah, her best friend Jenny, David, Justin, and another junior named Stephen, and each chipped in to buy Mitchell an Xbox game that was at the top of his Christmas list. None of the good Samaritans could drive at that time, so I loaded them into my vehicle, and we drove to Mitchell's house the day before Christmas Eve. Allie rang the doorbell, toting the gift bag and a batch of cookies she had made and decorated. Mitchell's parents answered the door, and seeing the small army of strangers on their doorstep, reluctantly ushered us in, probably concerned that Mitchell would be overwhelmed. The boy sat hunched on a couch in front of the TV staring at the floor as if contemplating the pile of the carpet. We were served hot chocolate and, while I made chit chat with Mitchell's parents, my daughters and their friends engaged him in conversation. I could barely hear his whispered speech, but by the time we left two hours later, he was laughing and joking with his visitors like an old friend.

Allie and her friends began a Saturday morning club called "coffee church," to which Mitchell was invited and faithfully attended. The group met at a hip coffee shop called Java Cat for the purpose of Bible study, but never actually studied the Bible. They brought their Bibles every week but admitted that it was really just a social event at which they consumed hot chocolate and pastries and goofed around. Mitchell abandoned his corner on the floor and began to sit with his new friends at the lunch table. He eventually joined the basketball, track, and golf teams, now happy and sociable and a darn good athlete to boot.

My point in putting our social worker through that long drama was this: If my daughters would go that far out of their way to love and welcome a lonely stranger, why would they reject their own baby sibling?

Suzanna, our social worker, was touched as we told the story of Martilena and our plans to adopt her. But she was well-versed in international adoption and expressed concern about

Guatemala's failure to comply with an international adoption treaty (The Hague Convention) and the resulting closure of the adoption programs between Guatemala and other countries, including the United States. We understood the situation but wondered if an exception could be made in our case, given our special connection with Martilena.

We made an appointment and traveled to Milwaukee to visit the U.S. Citizenship and Immigration Service which quickly put an end to our plans to adopt Martilena. No how, no way was the response we received. The door was shut and locked in terms of adoptions between the United States and Guatemala, and there was nothing we could do about it. We were sad and disappointed not as much for ourselves as for Martilena, but we had done what we could and had to concede that it was not God's will that she become our daughter.

It was time to look at the adoption programs of other countries. Latin America was our first choice because of our connection with the culture and our ability to teach our child his or her native language. Among those countries with adoption programs were Peru, Costa Rica, and Columbia, but each had requirements that eliminated us as adoptive parents. For example, one had a forty-five-year age limit for parents. Another required prospective adoptive parents to live in the country for two months, and yet another was offering only large sibling groups. We researched other countries of the world, carefully considering the limitations and travel requirements of each adoption program and eventually arrived on Russia as the perfect match for us.

There were many international adoption agencies handling adoptions from Russia, one of which was called Small Wings Adoption Foundation (SWAF). I established a rapport over the phone with then-Director Dinah Martinelli and appreciated the amount of time she spent after office hours one night explaining the process and the services of the foundation. The fees outlined in their contract were similar to those of other adoption agencies I had researched, so after having contacted their references, we signed a contract and began the application process.

The documentation and paper work required by Russia rivaled that of the 501(c)(3) process we had faced with the IRS. Forms were to be completed with meticulous accuracy, and all documents required notarization. Then each document required an apostille to authenticate the notarization. This process required numerous trips to the Wisconsin Secretary of State's office and proved to be extremely expensive as fees were charged for each apostille. It was an exhausting process that took months to complete. We were relieved when we had finally submitted the final documents and were officially in line for the referral of a child, which we were told could take up to a year and a half. It was time to return the focus of our attention to our work in Guatemala.

Chapter Twenty-One

A Labor of Love

Cleo Tindall was officially retired when she agreed to her role as Sponsorship Director. As the ministry grew, her administrative responsibilities increased greatly. She also attended board meetings and traveled frequently to Guatemala on team trips and, as a result, was working as a full-time volunteer in her retirement. She never complained, but in the spring of 2010, as we prepared to celebrate the five-year anniversary of the ministry, I thought about the load she was carrying and asked her how she was doing. She was fine, but I sensed she needed to be let off the hook at some point in the near future. Cleo was a highly-organized, detail-oriented leader. I had no idea who would fill her shoes, and the workload she carried would have cost the ministry thousands of dollars in terms of hired help. The training alone would be overwhelming. We prayed for God's provision.

Before we could lose sleep over the dilemma, my sister, Lauri Miro, stepped up and volunteered to carry the baton that

Cleo had carried for so many years. Lauri was the most highly-educated stay-at-home mom I had encountered to date. She was an RN and held an MBA as well as a degree in Hospital Administration. She had left her successful career years earlier to dedicate her time to her two young daughters, but remained involved in many volunteer activities through various organizations. Her children were now teenagers, and she felt she could phase out other volunteer responsibilities to dedicate her time to OWH.

During the transition, my dad worked feverishly, investing many hours of his time writing and implementing a computer program that would simplify the Sponsorship Program administration as well as our accounting process. I imagine this took place between midnight and 4 a.m., as he juggled the enormous work responsibilities and international travel necessitated by his recent developments in medical imaging. Together he and Lauri revised and streamlined our information management process and updated our donor lists and mailing procedures to save the ministry a great deal of time and money.

My mom (the indefatigable Darlene Mistretta) continued to serve as our treasurer, managing and recording what had become a seemingly endless ocean of receipts generated from administrative expenditures within the United States, and every seed, bean, and grain of rice purchased in Guatemala. Our auditors were constantly amazed at the accuracy and meticulousness of her records. The ministry had become one of God's relay teams with each team member carrying a different but important baton. Sponsors, churches, mission trip teams, staff members, prayer partners, and supporters were all vital to the ongoing operation of the ministry. The financial support of several faithful benefactors had been steadily increasing, enabling us to continue to implement new programs and give "yes" answers almost without hesitation to families in desperate need of specialized medical care.

Meanwhile back in Guatemala, Lucinda was showing serious signs of burnout. We encouraged her to rest more and take more time off, insisting that she post business hours on the office, which was still her home. At one point I suggested to Lucinda that we rent a second building to separate her home from the office, but she loved the security of the office building and the coming and going of the sponsored families.

We appreciated Lucinda and all she had done for the ministry and the people of Guatemala, but we sensed a discord between her and the other staff members. We could not get honest feedback about how things were going from our employees when interviewing them individually. They would simply say that everything was fine with tears in their eyes. Lucinda had resigned her position with us several times by this point, and each time she had changed her mind and decided to stay. We loved her and were grateful for her hard work and dedication, so each time she quit and then recanted we accepted her back. The instability was becoming stressful, however, as two hundred and seventy-five families depended on us for food, and multiple other programs were underway in addition to the Virtual Village and Life Boat Programs.

The joy of changing the life of another for the better is a fuel that powers the tireless efforts of those working long and unpredictable hours in ministries of every kind. I often imagine how tireless and steadfast we could be should we never face defeat. Unfortunately, not all stories have happy endings. One morning Lucinda called to inform me that Francina had moved her family back to her village and resumed life with her abusive alcoholic husband. This news was saddening to me but not nearly as crushing as the news of the following week. Our staff

learned that Oscar's mother had hired an attorney, and with a
new judge in place, had succeeded in legally removing him
from the orphanage. Oscar would now face another upheaval in
his life and a return to the dreadful situation from which we
had worked so hard to remove him. We wondered how on
earth a judge could have ruled in Sonia's favor given her track
record as a care provider. And we feared that she had fought for
the custody of her sons not out of love for them, but rather, out
of pride and the desire to "undo" the disgrace of having been
ruled incompetent as a parent.

We considered going to court to reopen the case and fight
for the return of the children to the orphanage, but the very
judge that had ruled in the mother's favor would have been
determining the outcome of our case. It was unlikely that she
would have overturned her own decision. We also knew that if
we went to war again in a custody battle with this family and
lost, we would forever alienate the mother and preclude any
chance of monitoring Oscar and supporting the family through
the Virtual Village program, which would be better than
nothing. We decided that our best course of action was to
attempt to befriend Oscar's mother with an invitation to attend
our sponsorship distributions. This way the family would
receive food and medical care and we would be able to assess
the health of the children once a month. To our extreme
surprise, she accepted. But after only a few months at home,
Oscar fell into severe malnutrition again. This time we were
able to convince his mother that he should be placed in
Dispensario Bethania, a private hospital in Jocotan that was a
step above the CRN and required payment which was covered
by OWH. Lab tests revealed that the entire family was infected
with giardia, an intestinal infection which we hoped was
responsible for Oscar's malnutrition in spite of adequate food

supplies. All were treated with antibiotics provided by OWH, and Oscar eventually returned home.

This season of bad news continued. Six months had passed since Alma's first surgery, and it was now time to take her to Guatemala City for an MRI to determine whether the Chiari Release procedure was successful in causing the cyst on her spinal cord to drain. The headaches she had suffered had all but disappeared indicating that the surgery had resolved her hydrocephalus. We were hopeful that the cyst had drained and we would be able to reschedule the scoliosis surgery, but this was not to be. The cyst remained. I was not in Guatemala when the results were received, a fact that spared me, but not Carol, the emotional distress of breaking the news to Alma and her family. Needless to say they were devastated. A disc of the MRI images was on its way to me, and I would forward it to Alma's surgical team and await a response.

February of 2011 marked Lucinda's fifth resignation, which came as a result of the board's refusal to honor her demand that we fire almost our entire staff. She had already fired seven employees during her five years as director. The board of directors unanimously approved my recommendation that this time we wish her well and accept her resignation with finality. I began the daunting task of identifying new leadership in Guatemala by posting the director position on the job posting sites of major Christian colleges in the United States. Although I listed fluent Spanish-speaking ability as a prerequisite, I received phone calls from a slew of unqualified candidates who spoke English, Chinese, and various other languages, but not Spanish. I had posted the requirement that the candidate relocate to Guatemala, but received calls from people either unwilling or unable to move. One candidate sent page after page of personal history revealing a dark past that had no place on a job application.

I am often referred to as a "Pollyanna" because of my unwarranted optimism in the face of seemingly hopeless situations, but at this point I was becoming discouraged. Disappointment over the recent streak of bad news and the growing responsibilities of directing the daily activities—both in Guatemala and the U.S—of a large international ministry began to take a toll on my health. I became a walking jug of Maalox and Excedrin and spent many sleepless nights wondering if I was still living out God's will for my life. Again I felt devoid of the peace and joy that Christians are promised through faith in Christ. I prayed for reassurance, renewed energy, and God's provision of a new leader that would carry a crucial baton in Guatemala, reminding myself that in spite of recent setbacks, we had made a difference for hundreds of families.

I bolstered my spirits envisioning thousands of children eating meals that they would not have had without our faithful sponsors. I thought of our medical teams and the countless lives saved through parasite treatment and the provision of other health care, the numbers of which we would never know. I thought of children at desks and computers where once there were none, and HIV patients still alive and healthy, thanks to the anti-retroviral treatments made possible by our supporters, and it occurred to me that God had never promised that this would be easy. He never promised easy victories or even lasting progress. Loving unconditionally requires a leap of faith with the knowledge that our efforts may never be rewarded by success, or even acknowledged with a simple thank you. We must choose to serve based on a higher reward—the knowledge that regardless of the outcome, we have offered our gifts of love and compassion to God and our fellow human beings expecting nothing in return. We must acknowledge that we are not in control and that our responsibility is only to make the effort, sometimes in vain, or possibly having planted seeds that will take root long after we leave this world. The rest is always up to God.

He had changed me, one challenge at a time, into something stronger, more hopeful, more tolerant, and more loving. I thought of Luis, the drunken villager who would have repulsed me had I encountered him before encountering Christ. I thought of the nights I had spent sleeping soundly in creepy insect-infested hotels. I thought of moments that should have terrified me but did not because of my faith in God for protection. And I thought of Terri Manthei, my maternal grandmother, whose walk with Christ had shaped her into His image to the greatest degree of any human being I had ever met. She could often be heard audibly talking to Him as if He were right there with her. On one occasion I almost found myself asking her how He was, as if she could give me an answer as to whether or not He was having a good day. Through her communion with Him she had become like Him, loving unconditionally and living selflessly to encourage and serve others. Having lost her husband to cancer years too early, her faith had never faltered. The example of my grandmother will always be a reminder to me that God is not finished working in me. In fact He has a very long way to go.

Chapter Twenty-Two

Transitional Heroes

Erica, who had been with us for three years at Lucinda's departure, was our longest term employee and had proven to be responsible and trustworthy. She agreed to serve as our interim director while I continued the search for new leadership in Guatemala. Alfredo Rodriguez, the husband of board member Wanda Rodriguez, became unemployed in the United States and volunteered to spend a month in Guatemala helping our staff during the leadership transition. Alfredo was 53 years old, of Puerto Rican decent, and spoke fluent Spanish. He frequently attended board meetings with Wanda and loved the ministry and Guatemala. Alfredo often referred to himself as "Fettucine," claiming he was named after the creamy Italian pasta dish. His quick-witted humor was balanced with a sense of responsibility and willingness to serve, and his sudden availability was a gift from God.

Darlene and I decided to travel to Guatemala with Alfredo to get him acclimated and to transfer the ministry bank account and administration from Lucinda to Erica. Alfredo purchased a GPS system, downloaded the mapping for Guatemala, and off we went. Darlene, Alfredo, Erica, and I spent the next few days revising legal representation documents and bank accounts and preparing Erica for the huge responsibility she would now assume. This shy, soft-spoken twenty-one-year-old woman would carry a heavy load in the months to come, and leaving the bank I remembered our first days in eastern Guatemala and the apprehension and feelings of inadequacy I had about beginning a ministry in this place. The three people at my side during this trip were a reminder to me that God had sent many helpers, and although the future was uncertain, we were not alone. Again the phrase "Onward Christian Soldiers" came to mind.

The trip had been productive, and we enjoyed a sense of peace and confidence as Alfredo loaded our luggage into the pickup truck for the four-hour trip back to Guatemala City. We were starting off later than we had hoped given the dangers of late night travel in Central America. Robberies and carjackings were common along the dark stretches of sparsely-traveled highway between the southeast corner of Guatemala and the capital city. But Darlene and I were to fly out early the next morning and had no choice but to make the trip. Alfredo programmed our Guatemala City hotel into his GPS, which he affectionately called "Stella." He locked the doors, and we were off. I dozed in the back seat of the double cab truck, tuning in and out of the light-hearted conversation and laughter of Darlene and Alfredo in the front seat. Three-and-a-half hours passed, and it occurred to me that we were not amid the billboards and increasingly commercial surroundings that should have lit the highway as we approached the city.

"Hey . . . Fettucine, we haven't heard from Stella in a while. Is she still awake?"

He laughed, fiddling around with the mechanism and adjusting its connection to the cigarette lighter.

"Recalculating, recalculating," came the voice of Stella as she suddenly sprang to life.

Alfredo reprogrammed the unit for our hotel, but the repeated "recalculating" was her only communication. The mood in the truck was rapidly changing. Something was wrong.

"She has no clue, Alfredo."

"Just wait, she's thinking." He defended his beloved Stella as if she were a faithful friend.

"Recalculating, recalculating," she mocked.

A few lights came into view as we neared what appeared to be a small township. Alfredo pulled off the highway knowing that asking directions of the wrong party at this hour could potentially place us in a "sitting duck" situation. We became aware that the dark green pickup truck that had been behind us on the highway had followed us off the main road. Alfredo made several redundant and illogical turns in an attempt to rid us of the trailing vehicle, which increased its distance but continued to follow us. As Alfredo circled aimlessly we tried to avoid panic. There was no safe public place to stop for help and proceeding out of the populated area and back down the desolate highway could have proven disastrous. A feeling of dread came over us and even the typically laid back and playful Alfredo was now somber and struggling to mask the sense of doom that he shared with his travel companions.

Another truck appeared in our rearview mirror, this one black with flashing blue lights, suggesting that we must have committed some sort of traffic violation. Alfredo pulled to the side of the road, and we prayed that this was indeed the police. Two uniformed men approached our vehicle, their flashlights illuminating the truck's cab. Alfredo, with his dark skin and hair, looked as if he could have been around the corner from his home, but Darlene and I felt like two fools in the wrong place at the wrong time. Still clinging to the hope that we were approaching Guatemala City, Alfredo asked for directions.

These were indeed police officers, but their response was not encouraging. "Do you mean the Guatemala City airport? Man, you are lost! You are in El Salvador." We had crossed the border long ago which explained why Stella had gone into a recalculating tail spin. She did not have the programming for El Salvador.

The two policemen apparently forgave us for driving the wrong way down a one-way street, a mistake that most likely saved us from the malicious intentions of the occupants of the green truck, which had now disappeared. They gave us lengthy directions for our return to Guatemala City, but in pitch darkness, and with no road markings, we were soon lost again, this time on a remote mountain highway, with no maps or electronic navigational assistance. It was a helpless feeling. Paranoia began to set in, and we questioned the honesty of the officers and the accuracy of the directions they had given. I wondered how much gas we had but didn't bring it up since there was nothing we could do about a possible shortage anyway.

My mom, still in the front seat with Alfredo, was as cool as a cucumber, probably refraining from hysteria for my sake. I felt homesick and, again, missed Randy. Suddenly I had an idea and wondered why I hadn't thought of it sooner. The basic Nokia phone I used in Central America was with me and fully charged. I texted my husband. "We need your help. We are lost in El Salvador."

Seconds later his reply came. "Very funny."

"I'm serious. We need you to get to a computer and Google map El Salvador."

The phone rang, and of course it was a very concerned Randy. The sound of his voice made me feel as safe as if I were in his arms. He was at his computer, and I passed the phone to Alfredo. Together they discussed the maps, retraced our path, identified our location, and planned our route. Randy stayed with us until we crossed back into Guatemala and Stella was able to take over. We arrived safely at our hotel in the wee hours of the morning, and I thanked God for His protection and modern technology, without which we might still have been driving aimlessly in the mountains of El Salvador.

Chapter Twenty-Three
An Unexpected Baton Carrier

Erica excelled as the ministry's temporary leader, and we considered promoting her to director, but when we asked her to serve as interim director she had said, "Yes, until you are able to hire a new director." We interpreted that to mean that she was not interested in playing this role for the long run. Furthermore, we acknowledged that her qualifications, like Lucinda's, were based on her love for the poor and willingness to serve, rather than solid education in administration and leadership. We feared she would soon face burnout and experience the same employee management difficulties that ultimately led to Lucinda's final resignation. We needed to be patient.

Early in March of 2011 I received a call from a young man named James Berkley. He had recently graduated from Wheaton College and was seeking a career in ministry. He had grown up in an American missionary family in Bolivia and therefore spoke fluent Spanish. As if that were not exciting enough, he went on to tell me that he was married to a young lady named Joy, who had just graduated from nursing school and passed her board exams to become an RN. It had been her dream since age five to become a missionary nurse.

The couple submitted formal applications and resumes, and we scheduled a conference call interview for them with the board of directors. We appreciated the friendly and loving personalities of James and Joy and were impressed by their servant hearts and willingness to sell their home and leave everything behind to begin life in Guatemala. We decided to take the next step. We invited them to join us in Guatemala for a tour of the region and our projects, giving them the opportunity to get to know us and our staff in Guatemala, and vice versa. They gladly accepted, and Randy and I were off to Guatemala to meet James and Joy Berkley.

The trip gave us a convenient opportunity to check on Oscar, and we made the journey to his home the day we arrived. I had not seen Oscar's mother since the night I had threatened to become her permanent house guest, and I knew I would likely not be welcomed with open arms. Images of Sonia pitching a fit and trying to run us out of the village crossed my mind, but Oscar had a solid grip on our heartstrings, and I decided it would be worth the risk of a confrontation to see how he was doing. I had heard that his mother's demeanor had improved and that she was now a far sight more pleasant. But I was not convinced that her new cordiality would apply to me. We traveled to his village, parked the truck, and began the descent down the path to Oscar's hut, armed as usual with toys for him, but this time also with a few household items as gifts for Sonia, who turned out not to be home. Oscar's grandmother was on hand as a caretaker for the children, and she tolerated our visit reluctantly. We enjoyed our time with our dear little friend and were relieved to find him in good health. Feeling satisfied that he was being fed and cared for, we thanked God for what appeared to be at least temporary stability in his life. Leaving the gifts for Sonia with Grandma, we returned to our truck and began our descent down the mountain.

Initially I had felt relieved to find that Sonia was not home, but now I was surprised to find myself feeling a twinge of disappointment about not having seen her. Maybe I was curious about whether she had indeed changed for the better. Or perhaps I subconsciously wanted to bring peace to the conflict that had been left unresolved since the dark, rainy night of the rescue mission. At any rate, I presumed she harbored nothing but hatred toward me. I did not have long to ponder these mixed emotions before becoming distracted by a familiar figure making its way up the road. It was Sonia. I fought off the childish instinct to duck before she saw me and blurted out, "Stop the truck." It was another of those decisions made without the luxury of even a moment to evaluate options and consequences. I jumped out of the vehicle, extended a hand to Sonia and said,

"Buenos Dias, Hermana."

She stared at me for a moment as if searching her memory, but then it clicked. In front of her was the woman who had threatened her with punishment from none other than God Almighty to persuade her to turn over her severely starved child for hospitalization against her will. My heart raced. Randy watched, listening from behind the wheel of the truck and wondering which of these times I would get in over my head to the point at which he would actually have to physically defend me. This was not to be the time. Sonia extended her hand, smiling as if happy to see me. I struggled to act as if I was not stunned, pretending that her warmth was to be expected. I told her we had visited Oscar and were happy to see he was doing well. Then the unexpected evolved into the extraordinary, proving that Sonia had overcome her bitterness about our having taken her son away in a bitter courtroom battle.

"A child in a neighboring village needs your help. Would you please come and see her?"

Randy and I exchanged glances, reading each other's minds.

"Is this really happening?" was the unspoken communication. And just like that she was in the truck, guiding us to the home of another child in need of help and hope in the form of food and medical care beyond the reach of her destitute family. Sonia signaled us to stop as we approached a grass hut, uncharacteristically dilapidated even for this region. A polite "Buenos dias" from Sonia was enough to summon a young woman from the hut, an emaciated child in her arms. In addition to her severe malnutrition, the five-year-old child could not walk due to a disability not easily diagnosed by me at a glance. Sonia spoke to the younger woman in a kind and caring tone as if she were an older sister giving advice to a sibling.

"I have brought help for Estella," she said. "These are friends from a ministry that saved the life of my son. They will help you too."

This was one of those moments when one simply must repress the geyser of tears that fights to erupt no matter the attempt to maintain composure. The woman would not have understood the emotional impact of the moment with no knowledge of the history between the members of this unlikely rescue trio. I needed to encourage the woman, explain the sponsorship program, and discuss medical care and possible physical therapy. It would not have been convenient to have become a blubbering sap. For once, I succeeded. The mother and child agreed to return to the office with us for profiling and arrangements for medical consultations.

Sonia thanked us as we dropped her off near her home on the way into town. I suddenly felt a bond with her that erased all past wrongs. Sometimes forgiving is difficult and requires conscious ongoing effort in the knowledge that the subject of our forgiveness will never change. This kind of forgiveness is required of those desiring to truly follow the teachings of Christ. Although it frees us from our own bitterness, it does not come as a result of the fact that all has been set right. But in Sonia's case it was easy. She had changed. I wondered if somewhere along the way she had accepted Christ and decided to follow Him—a step that is well-known for causing radical reform in the outlook and behavior of a human being. The opportunity for me to ask Sonia about her faith had not presented itself. It was a subject that I would have to discuss with my new friend at some time in the future. The one thing I did know was that she had become a baton carrier on God's relay team, swallowing her pride to connect a child with desperately needed help and hope by joining the team she had once opposed.

It was time to get back to the initial goal of this trip— giving James and Joy Berkley a tour of eastern Guatemala and the work of the ministry. The couple turned out to be a perfect fit. Although James was very tall and blond and stood out like a sore thumb in this land of dark-skinned people of short stature, we knew he would soon win the love and respect of the local population. Joy was equally tall and naturally pretty with dark hair and a personality that matched her name. The couple seemed to love Guatemala and the rugged beauty of the mountains, but more importantly, they were impressed with the work of the ministry and wanted to be part of it. They were offered the position as directors before boarding the plane for their flight home to New England. But there were details to be worked out.

We could offer only a meager salary, as is typical in ministry. They would need to raise support for their work from their home church, family, and friends, and they would need to find a buyer for their mobile home. As we parted ways, we asked them not to make a commitment to us immediately, but to take the time to think it over, talk between themselves, and pray for God's will. We wanted a minimum commitment of two years and did not want this young couple to make a hasty decision based on their first impression and the excitement of a great trip.

Having dropped the Berkleys at the airport in Guatemala City for their flight home, we spent a day in Antigua. Alfredo Rodriguez had finished his month volunteering in Chiquimula and had served the ministry well. He had traveled from Jocotan to Antigua with us, and we spent the day unwinding and listening to tales of the struggles he and the staff had faced in the wake of Lucinda's departure. Alfredo had clearly been through quite an ordeal. I had lived it with him by phone daily as he would call me often for advice and the contact information of ministry friends in Guatemala. Now, in the context of a happy ending and the anticipation of new leadership, we were able to laugh as we recalled the events.

Alfredo was relieved to be in the presence of Americans again. He missed his wife and was ready to go home. Randy and I expressed our gratitude for his service by treating him to dinner at an inviting candlelit restaurant lavishly adorned with tiny white lights. Alfredo, a professional drummer, performed as a guest for a few numbers with the Peruvian band that played festive music on a small stage near our table. We stayed late into the night, enjoying the fellowship and cheery ambiance, and laughing until we cried. This was one of those special nights that one wishes would never end.

We eventually made the trip back to an inexpensive hotel in Guatemala City where we planned to stay before catching an early morning flight home, but when we arrived we learned that we had lost our reservation because it was so late. We ended up at the only hotel still open in this relatively safe zone of the city—the Holiday Inn, Guatemala City. Alfredo came to our room for a beverage before turning in, and the stories continued. Alfredo has a contagious sense of humor that causes me to wonder if he missed his calling to become a comedian. He had us laughing so hard that the front desk was receiving complaints and called our room to ask us to be quiet. We tried. When the second call came in, we decided we had better call it a night before we became the first Christian missionaries to get kicked out of the Guatemala City Holiday Inn.

Chapter Twenty-Four

Eighty Pounds of Courage

Frozen Wisconsin farmland raced by the car windows on the final leg of our journey home from Guatemala City to Dallas to Chicago, and on to Verona, Wisconsin. We were exhausted but enjoying the last few hours of downtime before the frenzy of post-travel catch-up set in. I recognized the phone number appearing on my ringing cell phone as that of Dr. Noonan and assumed that because he was calling rather than using our typical electronic mode of communication, he had seen Alma's MRI results and didn't have the heart to tell me her dream was over by way of email. After his polite greeting came the grim acknowledgement, "It's still there."

But instead of the expected, "Well, at least we tried," Dr. Noonan said, "This will make things a bit more difficult."

He then went on to describe a complicated surgical scenario explaining that the best course of action would again begin with Dr. Iskandar and Dr. Bragg who would place a shunt to drain the spinal cord cyst, while at the same time fusing several vertebrae together to stabilize the upper spine. Fourteen days later Dr. Noonan would perform the scoliosis surgery to correct the curvature, with the possible need for yet a third surgery a week later to complete the process. The fusion procedure would require bone from Alma's hip for grafting between vertebrae, necessitating another incision and painful recovery site. The suffering that Alma would endure was difficult to fathom, but the brave young lady dreamed of something most of us take for granted—the ability to walk, run, sleep, and breathe normally, and to live the life of a healthy teenager.

The hospital administration stood by Alma as did the three surgeons and several anesthesiologists, each willing to make a much greater contribution than originally planned. I never learned the total value of the services that Alma would now be receiving as her needs mushroomed into several more surgeries and weeks in the Pediatric Intensive Care Unit, but I imagined that the number was astronomical. The outpouring of generosity was nothing short of miraculous. Alma gratefully accepted, this time without hesitation, and the surgeries were scheduled.

News of the miracle unfolding in Madison spread through the OWH support network while preparations were made for Alma's arrival. An army of volunteers joined the charge to make the experience as tolerable as possible for Alma and her parents. Anticipating the challenges of the language barrier, we could think of nothing more terrifying than lying in a hospital bed in excruciating pain, unable to communicate with medical personnel. Carol Langley would again travel with the family but could not be expected to provide support around the clock. I would be taking shifts, but recovery from the many surgeries would go on for weeks, and I was still saddled with the usual juggling act that was my life and an international adoption to boot. We knew we would likely be traveling back and forth to Russia during Alma's time in the United States.

Wanda Rodriguez stepped up to the plate in a big way by preparing a schedule and recruiting the help of Spanish-speaking Christian women from the Madison community, who volunteered to serve in shifts, and would provide translation coverage around the clock throughout Alma's time in recovery. By the day of the first surgery, the schedule was filled several weeks out, and OWH supporters had signed up to bring meals to the family and volunteers at the hospital. The kitchen cabinet assigned to the family at the Ronald McDonald House was loaded with snacks and portable meals. We were ready. Alma and her parents flew to Madison, completed the preoperative appointments and bided their time until the day of the first operation arrived.

After checking our brave young patient into her preoperative room, a flurry of activity kept her mind off the feelings of anxiety that understandably might have wrecked the nerves of anyone embarking on such a terrifying journey. Alma seemed inexplicably calm, but Roman was crying ceaselessly. We prayed together between the comings and goings of the medical team preparing Alma for surgery. Dr. Bragg and Dr. Iskandar each stopped in to greet and encourage Alma, and I thanked God not only for the talents and abilities He had given these two surgeons, but for their willingness to share their gifts as an act of selfless generosity.

Only one parent was to accompany Alma to the operating suite and stay with her until the anesthesia lulled her into unconsciousness. I wondered why Roman was chosen, since Juana was notably more composed. He suited up in blue scrubs, his hat and mask obscuring everything but his bloodshot eyes. We kissed Alma's forehead as she was wheeled off down the hall, and it was then that Juana's tears finally streaked her worried brown countenance. I often say that no one cries alone when I am around. This was no exception, and Carol joined in, the three of us embracing with the knowledge that later that day we would either be rejoicing over the report of a successful surgery or facing news that Alma was among the small percentage of patients that account for the risks spelled out in preparation for any procedure requiring general anesthesia and, in this case, neurosurgery. After seeing his daughter off, Roman returned and collapsed in a chair, head in hands, sobbing.

We were escorted to a cheery waiting room decorated with brightly-colored tropical fish. Parents and relatives of other patients worked crosswords and Sudoku puzzles to pass the time waiting for the outcome of their children's procedures. There is nothing one can do for a loved one in surgery other than wait and pray. Carol and I prayed constantly while Roman wandered back and forth in such a state of anxiety that I made a mental note of his need for a calming medication during the upcoming scoliosis surgery, which would be a much "bigger" and longer surgery involving a great deal more risk. The Sound of Music played on my laptop in Spanish, with Julie Andrews and her darling crew providing Roman with a welcome distraction from the task of pacing the floor. Carol emailed her prayer chain in Denver, and the OWH Board of Directors prayed from their homes, calling my cell phone frequently for updates. After what seemed like an eternity, Dr. Iskandar swept through the swinging door between the operating suites and the waiting room, the smile on his face revealing before words, that the surgery had been a success.

The days following that first surgery were difficult, as expected. Alma's face was swollen, her puffy eyelids obscuring the pain that eyes often reveal in spite of the bravest efforts of their owners. The after-effects of anesthesia coupled with narcotic pain medications caused nausea and vomiting which agitated her wound sites and intensified her pain. Alma's typically stoic demeanor was broken at times with anguished cries of pain. The thought of the rapidly approaching scoliosis surgery must have been horrifying to Alma who may have wished she could turn back, deciding that nothing could be worth this amount of suffering.

The Spanish-speaking volunteers were a Godsend. Each sat at Alma's side for hours at a time, stroking her hair and placing cool rags on her forehead, periodically translating her requests for position changes and additional pain medications. Carol covered the long daytime shifts with breaks from me when possible. Hospital interpreters appeared periodically for the conveyance of technical medical information, but could not provide the around the clock companionship made possible by Alma's team of angels offering comfort and reassurance during the long nights of agony. The dedicated group afforded Juana and Roman the opportunity to take breaks each day, during which they could return to the Ronald McDonald House for naps, showers, and real meals. It was difficult not to love this humble family, and the bonds of friendship that formed between the three of them and the volunteers will last a lifetime.

By the day before her first scoliosis surgery, Alma's pain had ebbed and she was smiling and visiting with her support team. The improvement offered her proof that pain does resolve with time, something she would have to remind herself frequently in the weeks to come. Dr. Noonan would take her apart and put her back together again, hopefully straighter, taller, and able to begin her new life. Morning finally dawned on the day that was a dream come true for Alma, but also a day she dreaded. We went through the now familiar routine in the preoperative room, this time with Roman under the calming effects of an Ativan tablet. Alma displayed her characteristic courage and positive attitude, while again Roman dressed in scrubs and held her hand as she was wheeled off to surgery.

Carol, Juana, and I watched Alma's gurney disappear down the hall surrounded by Dr. Noonan, an anesthesia team, and several operating room nurses. A group of doctors, nurses, and hospital employees that had come to wish Alma well remained in the hallway, one of which was a friend of my dad's and the head of the Department of Neurosurgery. Seeing our tears and obvious distress, he said, "Don't worry, she is in good hands. This is the 'A' team."

I could only nod politely, the lump in my throat preventing a response. His kind reassurance meant they had offered the best they had, the hospital's most capable crew, expecting nothing in return but the knowledge that they had remained committed to the goal for which they had chosen their professions—health and healing for all.

Eight hours passed slowly, interrupted periodically by reports from the operating room indicating that the surgery was progressing as planned. When afternoon became evening, the tropical fish waiting room closed for the day. We were moved to a small waiting room near the ICU suite that would be Alma's home following surgery. Hours nine, ten, and eleven ticked by, and there seemed to be a long gap in updates from the operating room. We prayed and paced the floor. Roman's tranquilizer had long since worn off, and he and Juana were growing increasingly worried and restless. Board members arrived one by one, joining us in prayer and offering unsubstantiated reassurance to Alma's parents. Twelve hours had passed, and hour thirteen was underway when Randy received a call from Dave Guif, his best friend. Dave had coincidentally been in surgery with Alma all day as the sales representative for Biomet, the company that had donated the orthotics. Dr. Noonan had not yet reached the waiting room when Dave, unable to contain his joy, blurted out, "The surgery went very well, and Dr. Noonan completed the entire correction today. There will be no need for another surgery."

Shouts of joy erupted from the crowd of supporters that filled the small waiting room. Some took to their knees in prayers of thanksgiving, while others hugged and cried tears of relief. When Dr. Noonan finally entered the room, Roman ran to him, throwing his arms around his waist and sobbing uncontrollably. "Gracias Hermano, gracias! Eres nuestro heroe. Que Dios le recompensa."

In a voice overcome with emotion and barely audible I translated, "Thank you brother, thank you! You are our hero. May God repay you."

The news was a long-awaited answer to many prayers and provided much encouragement, but in front of Alma remained the most difficult leg of the journey. She was wheeled to her room by a team of ICU nurses who engaged in a flurry of activity, connecting her to a web of tubes, wires, and monitors. To say that she did not look good would have been an understatement. Her face was swollen to the point of being barely recognizable, her skin gray from the prolonged anesthesia. Medical code language filled the room as nurses read off vital signs, oxygen levels, and other data measuring the stability or instability of Alma's condition. Carol, Juana, Roman, my parents, and I cramped into a corner of the room for fear of getting in the way during this crucial period of time, the urgency of the activity giving us the impression that Alma dangled precariously between life and death.

Those of us close to Alma have little memory of the first few days following that surgery, possibly due to repression or perhaps as a result of exhaustion. One of the few things I do remember is leaving the hospital with Carol at 3 a.m. one morning and becoming trapped in the hospital parking ramp. The automated arm that was to go up upon receiving payment was malfunctioning. We tried three different credit cards and were issued receipts and payment confirmation three times, but the arm would not budge. We were exhausted and at the same time punchy from the sleep deprivation and emotional stress of past days.

"I guess we'll just have to floor it and blast out of here," Carol declared, as if that were a perfectly acceptable plan.

"This dang hospital is providing hundreds of thousands of dollars worth of free services for Alma, but they are ripping us off on the parking!" I barked.

We laughed hysterically over the ridiculousness of that remark. We desperately needed rest and dreaded the idea of going back into the hospital to seek help. Luckily a parking attendant appeared out of nowhere, pushed a button, and instantly freed us before we got any nearer to acting on Carol's idea.

A continuous epidural drip mercifully delivered anesthesia to Alma's torso for the first stretch of her recovery, but the breathing tube it necessitated eventually seemed to become a bigger problem than the pain. Alma could communicate only by blinking and squeezing our hands, giving yes or no answers to our many questions. Tears rolled toward her ears while she gagged on the tube, her eighty-pound body tethered to the bed that had become her hellish prison. The pain of her broken bones and incisions was coupled with sharp spasms caused by her newly repositioned muscle tissue. At times she appeared so pitifully miserable that her helpless volunteer companions would have to leave the room, themselves crying, to return later after having regained their composure. Respiratory complications arose due to Alma's immobility, and at one point we were informed that her left lung had collapsed. A pediatric pulmonary specialist joined Alma's medical team, and we redoubled our efforts to recruit the prayers of our supporters. Pulmonary therapy began, and churches throughout Madison prayed together for Alma. Flowers, balloons, and baked goods flooded her room, as well-wishers rallied to encourage the brave little fighter.

The days following surgery turned into weeks. Tubes and wires were removed gradually as Alma recovered. One day, rather abruptly, she turned a corner and appeared to fight harder than ever toward her discharge—the light at the end of this very long tunnel. It seemed to hinge on a specific solitary event—a bath. She was hoisted from her hospital bed by two nurses, causing excruciating pain, but offering a pivotal step toward normal. This familiar daily ritual, usually taken for granted, gave Alma the hope that she would soon add other normal activities to her routine until she was finally able to return home triumphant and living her dream of life without debilitating scoliosis. She would become living proof that when inextinguishable hope meets self-sacrificial love, miracles occur.

Chapter Twenty-Five

With Love From Stavropol

The Berkleys officially accepted the directorship shortly
after they returned home from their first trip to Guatemala.
The board of directors was elated and viewed this news as an
answer to prayer. Erica continued to lead the ministry
beautifully as interim director while they prepared for their
move, and all was well. Darlene and I made another
administrative trip to Guatemala that spring to accomplish
various business related tasks and to begin the search for a
living situation for James and Joy. This time it would be
separate from the office. It was during our layover in Houston
returning from that trip that I read an email from Small Wings
Adoption Foundation on my Blackberry. The subject line read
"With Love from Stavropol."

Attached to the email were the photos of two beautiful
Russian children named Anya and Yuri. They were siblings who
had been neglected by their severely alcoholic mother. Her
parental rights had been terminated, and they had been

classified as orphans and placed for adoption. The children were represented as being healthy. Anya was a blond three-year-old toddler with bright blue eyes and an angelic face. Yuri was one year old and as cute as could be. His darling round face and coarse brown hair brought to mind the image of a koala bear. Excitement grew as my mom and I gazed at the photos, imagining these precious children as members of our family. I forwarded the photos to Randy who was as excited as we were, in spite of concerns over the additional costs associated with raising not one but two additional children. We were invited to Russia to meet the children.

The process required leaving almost immediately, as children not accepted quickly are soon referred to other prospective parents. We applied for expedited Russian visas and booked our flights from Chicago, to New York, and on to Moscow. Our visas arrived by FedEx four days later, which was the day we left for Chicago. The adoption process required parents to make two trips to Russia, the first of which was to meet the children and to spend one or two hours with them on each of three consecutive days. Parents who wished to go forward were then to sign papers accepting the referral and return home to await a court date for which they would return to Russia to finalize the adoption, usually several months later.

Upon arriving in Moscow we were exhausted and jet lagged. We were met by Boris, a blond-haired, blue-eyed representative of SWAF who was to act as our translator and guide. We had several hours to kill before boarding our two-hour domestic flight south from Moscow to Stavropol, so Boris suggested we visit popular tourist sites such as the Kremlin and Red Square. But we were cold and tired and not dressed for an outdoor walking tour. It was late spring but the temperature in Moscow was in the low thirties. We ate lunch and spent most of our time at Shpakovskoye Airport which handled domestic flights within Russia. Upon parting ways with Boris in Moscow, he announced that we owed him $130 for his services, which we would be expected to pay on any day that we came into contact with him throughout the adoption process. We had already paid $25,600 to SWAF, $14,000 of which were "foreign country fees" and were to have covered interpretation and all required services within Russia for the completion of the first portion of the adoption. SWAF would require another $16,000 in "foreign country fees" before the finalization of the adoption. We guessed that Boris's demand for money was an error resulting from a communication breakdown, so we paid him to avoid an awkward situation, assuming we could rectify the misunderstanding with SWAF later.

The rickety, run down plane we boarded for our flight to Stavropol was most likely built in the 1950s. As the plane rattled and clanked down the runway, many of the luggage compartment doors swung open, and the "fasten seatbelt" signs and cabin lighting flickered on and off. It was one of those Twilight Zone moments during which life feels somehow surreal, as if part of a dream. We might have been afraid, but we remembered the many times we had feared for our lives on narrow muddy roads bordering river gorges in Central America. Surely God did not need to bring us to Russia to do us in if our number was up. We were served a meal that consisted of a sliver of raw fish, a dinner roll, a slice of hard salami, and a prepackaged Russian cookie of some sort.

It was late when we arrived at the small dingy airport in Stavropol—a scene that reminded us of an old black-and-white movie. Jet bridges were part of a world we had long since left behind, and the walk from the stairs of the airplane to the dimly-lit one-room reception area seemed eternal because of the cold and wind. An archaic circular baggage carousel squeaked laboriously as it rotated, its comically small size causing me to wonder what purpose it actually served. We waited for the woman who was to be our guide and translator in Stavropol, watching our fellow passengers engage in emotionless greetings and disappear to waiting vehicles.

Before long we were the only people left in the airport, which would soon be closing. A feeling of dread came over me. We were in the middle of nowhere in a country where I barely spoke the language. I had learned enough Russian to order food and make polite conversation, but that did not make me feel any better about our situation. I imagined that we would soon be forced out into the cold without a working cell phone or any hope of calling a taxi or even communicating what we were doing there. No one spoke a word of English. Finally a woman arrived and identified herself as Svetlana, our SWAF representative. A driver named Edgar waited nearby in a small, tired looking Russian-built vehicle, and we were whisked off to a hotel. We collapsed into deep sleep for the few hours we had before being picked up at 6 a.m. for a three-hour car ride to a remote orphanage in rural Stavropol, Russia.

Edgar and Svetlana picked us up as planned, and the four of us were to spend six hours each day for the next three days en route to and from the orphanage where Yuri and Anya lived. Stavropol is in the southwest corner of Russia, two hours south of Moscow by air. The landscape in April was frozen, desolate, and uninviting. The small dilapidated dwellings that occasionally came into view along the lonely highway appeared uninhabited and abandoned. We huddled in the back seat of the cold, drafty vehicle; unfamiliar Russian music playing as we drifted in and out of sleep. Today was the long awaited day we would meet the children we hoped to adopt, but oddly the excitement we should have felt more closely resembled apprehension.

The orphanage was a pleasant surprise—clean, colorful, well-staffed, and stocked with toys. We were led to a conference room where we were to meet with the medical director who would share the children's detailed health history. The tall neatly groomed woman began with Anya. "She occasionally begins to shake and then passes out, and her skin turns blue," came the translation from Svetlana. "She is on four anti-convulsive medications to control her seizure disorder." The doctor went on to state that Yuri had cerebral palsy and hepatitis C, an incurable liver disease that often requires a liver transplant. Upon meeting the children it was clear to us that both had fetal alcohol syndrome. We were only allowed to glance at Yuri from across the room, which was a great disappointment to us after having traveled halfway around the world to spend time with him. We were allowed to play with Anya for about twenty-five minutes before Svetlana abruptly began putting the toys away stating that the child was getting "overexcited," and it was time for us to go.

By the time we reached our hotel room we were reeling with emotions—disappointment, anger, anxiety, and a broken-hearted sadness for the children whose impairments resulted in large part from their mother's alcohol use. They deserved a loving family, but we were not sure it was to be ours. We were emotionally invested in the children and already had a crib and toddler bed set up for them in a nursery our daughters had beautifully decorated. We wanted to put our "better judgment" aside and take them home to give them the love and special care they desperately needed. But this time the Pollyanna in me did not win.

We received the children's medical records in English and immediately forwarded them to our daughters' pediatrician, requesting her analysis as quickly as possible. Although it was late afternoon in Russia, it was early morning in Wisconsin, and we received her response that evening. It was not encouraging. Her analysis of the health conditions of the children was followed by these words:

> In summary, it looks like both children have very challenging medical issues in addition to their developmental delays. Adopting one or both of them would significantly change your lives and would likely require the involvement of multiple specialists, multiple medications, and possibly worsening disease despite the best care available (at least for Yuri). Sometimes seizures can be controlled and sometimes they cannot be controlled, so even Anya could have medical issues that the best care cannot bring under control.
>
> Please call me at the office if you would like to discuss this further.
>
> Susan Metcalfe

Could it possibly have been God's will that we adopt not one, but two severe special needs children, thereby putting an end to our ability to travel back and forth to Guatemala? We felt betrayed by our adoption agency which had portrayed Anya and Yuri as healthy children. Clearly the poor health of the children was well-documented. Why had it not been shared with us before we traveled such a great distance to meet them? Could we provide the kind of attention these children needed considering our many commitments? Yuri and Anya might never reach independence. Didn't they deserve younger parents who would be with them well into adulthood? Randy was experiencing physical symptoms of stress that served as a clear indication to me that adopting these children was not in their best interest or the best interest of our family. They needed and deserved more than we could give.

We spent most of that night crying and praying between periods of restless sleep. By morning we had come to terms with the fact that there are families specifically called to parent special needs children, and there are families called to serve the poor in Guatemala, but usually not both simultaneously. God had already given us tremendous responsibility in roles we were certain He had planned for us. We were aware that one of the most serious mistakes a servant-hearted Christian can make is to assume that every service opportunity that arises is his or hers to accept. Each of us has a limited number of hours in a day and a limited amount of emotional energy. By spreading ourselves too thin, we deny God the full measure of ourselves that *He* intended for *His* purpose and calling for our lives.

The next day we visited the children one more time, praying constantly for God's affirmation that accepting these children was not His will for our lives. We knew that if we declined, they would forever be in our hearts, and we would always wonder about them. As difficult as it was, we signed the papers refusing the referral of Yuri and Anya and returned to our hotel room to collapse from physical and emotional exhaustion. Before long there was a knock on the door. It was Olga, an attorney that represented SWAF clients and was to guide us through the adoption process. We did not have a great deal of trust in any of the representatives of SWAF by now, but Olga was a breath of fresh air. She entered our room with Svetlana, who translated her introduction. She had heard about our situation and wished to encourage us. She explained that she had called in a favor and arranged for us to meet a baby boy that could not officially be offered until a few weeks later, as children in Russia are required to be available for domestic adoption for eight months before becoming available for international adoption. The baby was in a local orphanage very near our hotel, and Olga was offering to arrange for us to meet him the following day. We accepted her offer and began to feel mildly encouraged.

The following day we met the little boy who would become our son, Carson Randal Tews. At only ten-months old he was curious and playful and laughed easily. He looked as if he could have been our biological child, and we quickly fell in love with him. We had not seen the sun since arriving in Russia, but at the moment he was placed in our arms, the sun shone through the orphanage window as if a sign from God. The child had been born eight weeks premature, and there were health issues associated with his history, but we felt we could offer him the care he needed while fulfilling our responsibilities at home and in Guatemala. We gave our verbal acceptance of the child and packed our bags to return home. Since this trip could not be counted as the official trip to meet the child, the entire journey had to be repeated to fulfill the three-day meeting requirement after he was officially available for adoption.

Parting ways with our translator and driver, each demanded a large sum of money for their services, which were also specifically listed as included in the thousands of dollars we had already paid to SWAF in foreign country fees. Upon returning home, Small Wings Adoption Foundation was sympathetic about our ordeal in Russia and refunded a portion of the money their employees had demanded, but the requirements of money outside of what the contract specified continued throughout the process. In hopes of preventing other couples from having the same experience, we reported their practices to several agencies governing adoption practices and ethics.

Chapter Twenty-Six

Treasures in Heaven

❧

As 2011 wore on, so did the recession. One of our rental properties on Madison's west side had been vacated by long-term tenants who left the four-bedroom house in a state of wreck and ruin. We could not sell or rent it without investing $30,000 in repairs and renovations. Our daughter, Allie, was graduating from high school, and during better financial times, we had promised her some sort of used vehicle as a graduation gift. The adoption would now require three trips to Russia between April and August. It would not only cost us thousands of dollars in airline tickets, hotel rooms, and other travel expenses, but would result in a total of six weeks in Eastern Europe and away from work. That combined with the four weeks of travel to Guatemala in the spring of 2011 totaled ten weeks away from income-generating activities during the busiest months for real estate sales.

Upon returning home from our first trip to Russia I scrambled to catch up with OWH ministry business both at home and in Guatemala. My time was consumed with making reservations and planning the agenda and activities for the upcoming twenty-eight member June mission team, making arrangements for the transfer of leadership from Erica to James and Joy, contracting the renovations of the income property in order to sell it, planning a graduation party for Allie, and preparing paperwork and gathering documentation for our upcoming adoption court date.

I was a wreck, not over my "to-do" list, but because of the worry that resulted from our financial situation. I now knew first hand how closely one's sense of well-being could be linked with one's financial picture when money was scarce. Our struggle gave me a new understanding and empathy for the millions of hard-working Americans who were losing their homes through no fault of their own during the ongoing recession. I imagined my family running out of money completely and envisioned what it must be like to be among the millions of families in Guatemala and around the world living on less than a dollar a day, some unable to feed their children. It is often said that money can't buy happiness, but we kid ourselves if we do not admit that the extreme lack of it is a hindrance to happiness, health, and even survival. The enjoyment of life requires sufficient resources to meet at least basic needs and can be enhanced by the blessing of a small surplus. On the other hand, the excessive and all-consuming pursuit of wealth destroys happiness when it becomes an idol and requires the sacrifice of time otherwise spent on love—for our children, spouses, parents, friends, and God.

Our financial decline led us to believe that we had somehow gotten it wrong, skewing the delicate balance and dangerously tipping the scales in the wrong direction. We wondered if it had been a mistake to begin the adoption process, and once again, doubts about God's goodness and omnipotence crept into my mind. I had been serving Him as a volunteer for eleven years and had all but given up my career to care for those in need. We had willingly given up the lifestyle we had been living before we started to serve God and were now praying, not for great riches, but for just enough to meet our obligations. But the more we prayed for God's provision, the more we felt unheard and abandoned. Maybe I felt we deserved a break as a reward for our efforts on God's behalf. We reached a point prior to our final trip to Russia at which we feared we might not be financially able to complete the adoption, in which case, all invested to this point would be lost and our dream of parenting again would be shattered. I wondered if God heard our prayers for provision and simply chose to ignore them. If He truly was omnipotent and could have provided, why hadn't He? Was it His will that we live in this constant state of stress and worry?

As Christians we are taught that God is to be worshipped and praised, and indeed He is. But this sometimes prevents us from being honest with one another about our struggles and doubts, which in turn robs us of the support and encouragement of our fellow Christians. This is especially true for those in leadership positions. As ashamed as I was of my feelings, I dared to share them with a Christian mentor. I compared God as my Father, with myself, as Allie's parent.

"Suppose my beloved child, Allie, told me that she was going to give up her career, and instead of earning lots of money, she was going to devote her life to serving me and my loved ones in need. And suppose Allie did that for many years and eventually reached a point at which she needed my financial help. What kind of parent would I be if I had all the resources imaginable but would not answer her pleas, not for luxuries, but for just enough to get by, while she continued to serve me?"

I was on a roll and my pity party felt well-deserved. It seemed as if we were being punished for serving Christ. Although I prayed for unwavering faith, God had given us logic and the ability to reason, and nothing was making sense to me. In all honesty, I began to resent God for turning a blind eye to our needs, as we worked so hard to meet the needs of others. But I was tired of the whining that was going on in my heart. I missed and much preferred the "Pollyanna" in me and knew that those qualities—hope, optimism, and a positive attitude— were consistent with the teachings of Christ.

Somewhere in the midst of these struggles and this season of anger, I could not help loving Him who had led us on this journey and had been with us on every mountainside. I could not ignore the gratitude I felt for the experiences that had shaped our hearts and lives. Each struggle had prepared us for the next, more challenging situation, some of which, had they occurred out of sequence, would have seemed insurmountable. In my heart I knew that God had blessed us immensely. The small sacrifice we had made was miniscule in comparison with what Christ's missionaries, martyrs, and faithful followers had faced throughout the ages. I began to understand that what we had given up was rubbish compared with the immeasurable riches we had gained.

I recalled hearing of a businessman that earned nearly a thousand dollars per hour. In our culture this man would have been considered highly important and successful. I remembered our early years of climbing the ranks in real estate, pursuing not only high income, but the prestige and respect that came with success in one's field. I wondered what an hour of our time had been worth in those days. How differently we had come to view value. Events played through my mind like the frames of a film as I recounted an hour we had spent at a dump in Guatemala feeding families that had been digging through rotting trash in competition with vultures for food. I watched Danny, our youngest team member, handing out sandwiches, juice boxes, and toys to hungry children, and it occurred to me that in God's economy, this hour of an eight-year-old boy's time was worth far more than an hour spent by the highest paid professional. Jesus hailed the value of something as simple as giving a child a cup of water. Each act of kindness, no matter how small, is noticed and appreciated by Him, and the rewards come in terms of treasures in heaven, not provision in this world.

We are not all called to give all we have to live on, as did the widow in Jesus' parable—or to sell all we have and follow Him, as He told the rich man to do. But that should not stop us from changing the world one kind deed at a time, wherever we are and with whatever we can spare. It simply will not do to be frozen under a spell of helplessness in the face of the tremendous need in the world, or to be evasive about the opportunities before us because of the guilt we feel in the knowledge that we are not doing enough. If each of us gave only enough of our time and resources to feel the slightest pinch of sacrifice, there would not be one hungry child, and every village would have clean drinking water. There is no place to hide from the reality that thousands of children die each day that we, even as individuals, have the power to save.

That which breaks our hearts and brings forth our tears ought to compel us to act to incite change. The voice in our hearts can be quieted, but not silenced, by distractions and apathy. If we are honest, we must acknowledge that batons not carried leave the gaps through which are falling our sisters, brothers, nieces, and nephews in humanity. Until we have exhaled for the last time, it is not too late to make the difference that will change the world for even one. The hurt that each of us has experienced has sown compassion in our hearts and prepared us for something awesome. Have you, like Allie, felt ridiculed and lonely? There is someone like Mitchell in need of your love, encouragement, and acceptance. Have you struggled with addiction and rejection? You are living proof to someone like Luis that victory is attainable. Plant the seeds of hope for someone, somewhere, and take your place on God's relay team.

> [34] *"Then the King will say to those on his right, 'Come, you who are blessed by my Father; take your inheritance, the kingdom prepared for you since the creation of the world.* [35] *For I was hungry and you gave me something to eat, I was thirsty and you gave me something to drink, I was a stranger and you invited me in,* [36] *I needed clothes and you clothed me, I was sick and you looked after me, I was in prison and you came to visit me.'*
>
> [37] *"Then the righteous will answer him, 'Lord, when did we see you hungry and feed you, or thirsty and give you something to drink?* [38] *When did we see you a stranger and invite you in, or needing clothes and clothe you?* [39] *When did we see you sick or in prison and go to visit you?'*
>
> [40] *"The King will reply, 'Truly I tell you, whatever you did for one of the least of these brothers and sisters of mine, you did for me.'* (Matthew 25: 34-40)

Afterword

James and Joy Berkley assumed their roles as the Directors of Outreach for World Hope in Guatemala in June of 2011. They brought with them an attitude of humility and a desire to learn the culture and collaborate with partner ministries, medical personnel, and government officials, thereby making many friends and serving as excellent ambassadors for Outreach for World Hope. They are cherished by the ministry family and the communities of Guatemala as they love and serve God and our brothers and sisters in need. With their leadership, the ministry is beginning new programs such as the installation of latrines, adult career training, and scholarships for school-age children as a stepping stone to a brighter future. We are overjoyed to be working alongside this servant-hearted couple and eagerly look forward to what God has in store for the years to come.

Stavropol, Russia, proved to be a beautiful and inviting town during our second trip to spend time with Carson in June of 2011. The adoption was completed on July 29th, 2011, and our son was welcomed into his loving extended family upon traveling from Russia to the U.S. in August of 2011, on the day after his first birthday.

Spring of 2012 marked the beginning of the end of the season of drought in the real estate market. Randy and I were finally able to see the light at the end of the tunnel and enjoy the sense that we had weathered the storm and emerged stronger than ever before with the knowledge that the joy and fulfillment we had experienced during our eleven years in ministry were worth far more than financial security or any material provision God could have offered us. We, as Christians, have the assurance that no matter what we face in this world, our story has a happy ending. We have found the pot of gold at the end of the rainbow in Jesus Christ, and the best is yet to come for us. This is the message of hope we offer to those we serve, and this is the blessed assurance that we as Christians can hold on to. We would not trade the past eleven years for all the riches on earth and would do it all again if it were the year 2000 and we were invited to Ecuador while on a van ride in Mexico. It is with joy and gratitude that we will lead the Outreach for World Hope ministry into the future.

Please visit www.outreachforworldhope.org for updated information on the work of OWH.

A wise woman who was traveling in the mountains found a precious stone in a stream.

The next day she met another traveler who was hungry, and the wise woman opened her bag to share her food. The hungry traveler saw the precious stone and asked the woman to give it to him. She did so without hesitation. The traveler left, rejoicing in his good fortune. He knew the stone was worth enough to give him security for a lifetime.

But a few days later he came back to return the stone to the wise woman.

"I've been thinking," he said, "I know how valuable the stone is, but I give it back in the hope that you can give me something that is far more precious. Give me what you have within you that enabled you to give me the stone."

Author Unknown

Map of Guatemala

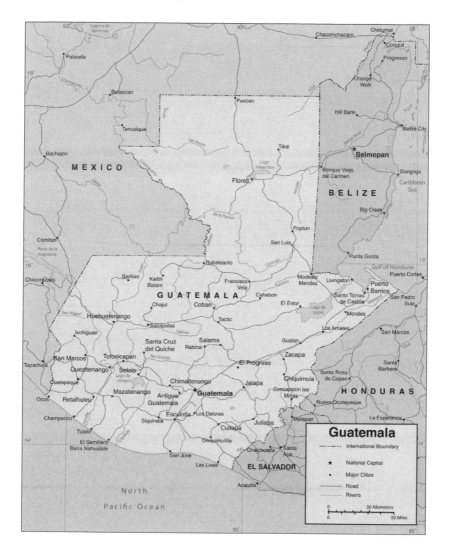

195

Photo Album

Elias arriving at CRN   *Elias before Rehabilitation*

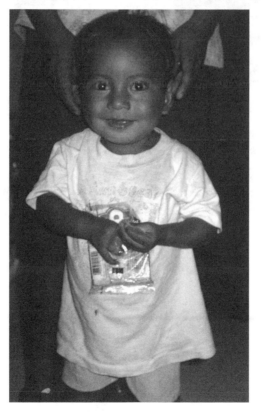

Elias after Rehabilitation

Lidia receives a gift from her child sponsor
after nutritional rehabilitation

Darlene and Charles Mistretta

Kim Tews and brother, Scott Mistretta

Kim and Randy with sponsored family through AOJ

Kim Tews and mom, Darlene Mistretta, 2005
First trip to Eastern Guatemala

Steep, dry, rocky conditions make food production difficult

Kim Tews and sister, Lauri Miro, en route to Guatemala

Allie and Leah Tews, 2008

Volunteer team awaits flight to Guatemala

Jim Farina and Lloyd Tindall at newly-installed bucket kit garden

Bucket kit garden three weeks after installation

Tews Family, Summer 2009

OWH volunteer medical team at mobile medical clinic

Village families gather for mobile medical clinic

Randy shaves heads to eliminate lice

Kim Tews and Cleo Tindall at 2010 supplies distribution

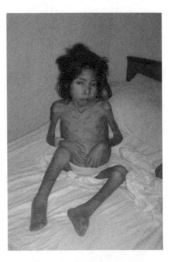

Rita at private hospital

Rita after rehabilitation

Kim and Randy in Naples, FL

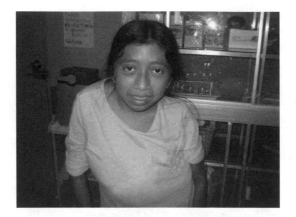

Alma at OWH office in Jocotan
seeking sponsor for scoliosis surgery

Alma's spine before scoliosis surgery

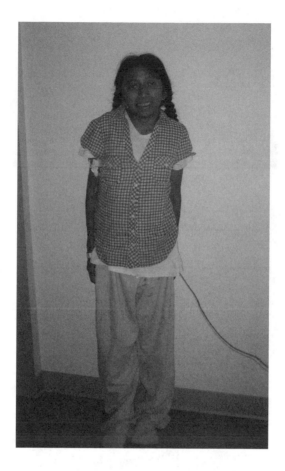

A new Alma Xiomara Morales Diaz

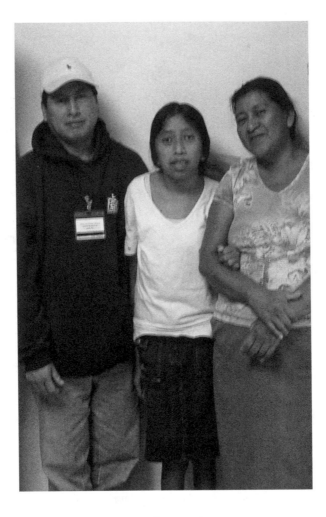

Roman, Alma, and Juana

Carson Randal Tews

Send This Book To A Friend!

To order please visit
www.tearswatertheseedsofhope.com